The German Baking Book

Jürgen Krauss

The German Baking Book

Cakes, Tarts, Breads, and More
from the Black Forest and Beyond

weldonowen

weldon**owen**

an imprint of Insight Editions
P.O. Box 3088
San Rafael, CA 94912
www.weldonowen.com

CEO Raoul Goff
VP Publisher Roger Shaw
Editorial Director Katie Killebrew
Senior Editor Karyn Gerhard
VP Creative Chrissy Kwasnik
Designer Megan Sinead Bingham
VP Manufacturing Alix Nicholaeff
Production Manager Joshua Smith
Sr Production Manager, Subsidiary Rights Lina s Palma-Temena

Weldon Owen would also like to thank Margaret Parrish and Jon Ellis for their
work on this book.

First published in Great Britain in 2023 by Kyle Books
An imprint of Octopus Publishing Group Limited
Carmelite House
50 Victoria Embankment
London EC4V 0DZ
An Hachette UK Company
www.hachette.co.uk

ISBN: 979-8-88674-061-5

Manufactured in China by Insight Editions
10 9 8 7 6 5 4 3 2 1

Insight Editions, in association with Roots of Peace, will plant two trees
for each tree used in the manufacturing of this book. Roots of Peace is an
internationally renowned humanitarian organization dedicated to eradicating
land mines worldwide and converting war-torn lands into productive farms
and wildlife habitats. Roots of Peace will plant two million fruit and nut trees
in Afghanistan and provide farmers there with the skills and support necessary
for sustainable land use.

Introduction

Imagine a small, square room. You enter it through the door set close to its left corner. From the doorway, you look through the big window, with a view onto the brook, and a steep, overgrown hillside with the ascending road to the church carved into it. You can also see the bricked-up entrance to a tunnel, a bomb shelter that was never used and is now home to bats. Running below the level of the window and along the left wall nestles a corner bench, the boxes under the seats offer practical storage for newspapers and children's books. Between the bench and the door is the wooden table. It is small, but expandable.

Within this small, square room, propped against the remaining walls, you will find a coal-fired oven and an electric stove, a sink and a cupboard. You are in the crowded kitchen of my childhood, where my brother and I played, the whole family ate, I did my homework, and my mother cooked and baked. This was the center of my early childhood in Germany.

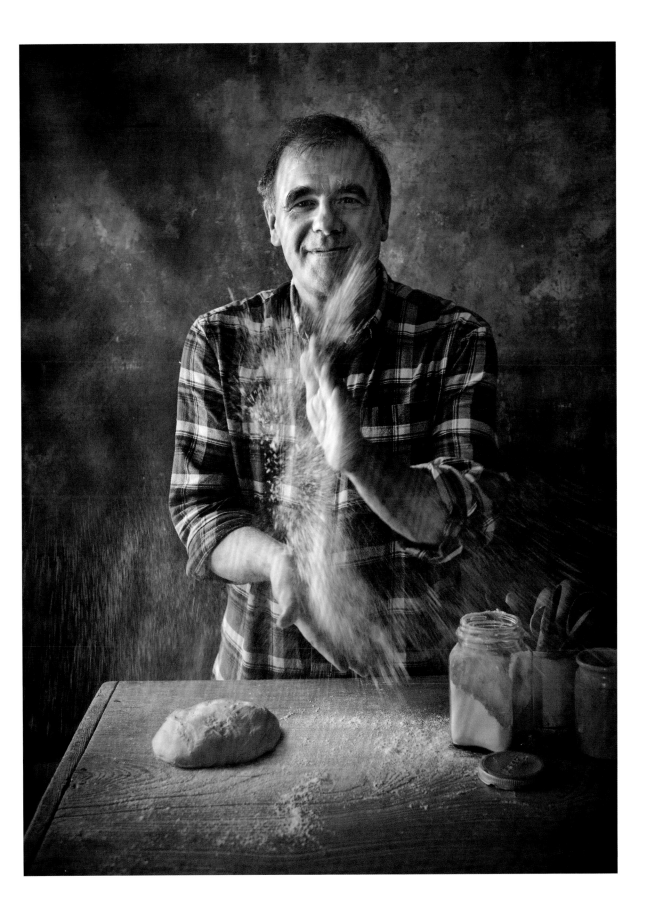

In such a close space it is inevitable that everybody gets involved in everybody else's activities, and, therefore, I am sure that I got my hands into dough as soon as I could stand up, even if I don't have memories of the event.

During the year we would bake cheesecakes, marble cakes, Linzer Torte, but the time everybody in the household looked forward to most of all was Advent. In November, we would start baking Christmas cookies together, a hugely fun and messy activity. I remember making glazed shortbread cookies, decorated with sprinkles. My mother was always kind and let my brother and me do what we wanted, which resulted in completely overworked dough and cookie monstrosities that never really baked all the way through!

My baking continued through my teenage years, with occasional Linzer Torte, plum tarts, and cheesecakes, but I never thought of making layered cakes or bread. The desire to make bread, specifically bread as it was sold in our neighbor's store, emerged sometime after I had moved to the UK, where I found that there were excellent books about breadmaking on the market.

By the time I applied for *The Great British Bake Off,* I was a confident bread-baker and had branched into baking cakes and tarts as well. Unexpectedly, my participation in the show reconnected me strongly to the sweet aspects of my past, and I found myself able to develop recipes for many classic delicacies that our family used to buy from bakeries, as well as the cakes and cookies we used to make in that small kitchen. Many of those recipes have now become favorites of my family in England. This is what this book is all about.

I invite you to accompany me through the flavors of my life in Germany. I hope you enjoy the journey.

MY MOTHER HOLDING ME. SHE IS STANDING IN THE COURTYARD,
WHICH HADN'T CHANGED SINCE SHE WAS A CHILD, AND IT WAS
ALSO THE PLAYGROUND OF MY CHILDHOOD.

Waffles, crepes, and dumplings

Crepes were always a quick after-school lunch in my home. Usually, we had them savory, with mushrooms and a white sauce. I won't include the standard crepes recipe here because I trust the reader to have their own great recipe. But there are many related recipes popular in Germany, and the collective word for them is Mehlspeise, food made with flour, and in this chapter, I present some family favorites.

Apfel-Küchle
Apple Fritters

Up until the age of fifteen, there were no afternoon classes, and my school didn't have a cafeteria. Therefore, my brother and I returned home from school hungry between 12:30 and 1:30 p.m., depending on our schedules. My poor mother did what she could to have lunch ready for us, but sometimes that didn't work out, and Apfel-Küchle was a welcome lunch on those occasions.

The three of us got busy in the kitchen together: one of us would peel and core the apples; one of us would slice the apples, and one of us would prepare the batter. A very quick, sweet lunch was prepared in record time.

The apples need to be a bit firm after cooking, so I like to use tart, firm apples, such as Granny Smith.

serves 4 as a dessert

2 LARGE FIRM, TART APPLES,
SUCH AS GRANNY SMITH

1 CUP (100G) ALL-PURPOSE FLOUR

2 MEDIUM EGGS

1 PINCH SALT

½ CUP (100ML) WHOLE MILK

VEGETABLE OIL FOR FRYING

CINNAMON SUGAR FOR SPRINKLING
(page 181)

Peel and core the apples. Cut the apples into slices perpendicular to the core, so that you get apple rings. If you don't have an apple corer, cut the slices first and use a sharp round object, like a piping nozzle, to remove the core from each slice.

To prepare the batter, put flour, eggs, salt, and milk into a bowl and mix to form a thick, smooth batter.

Heat some oil in a frying pan over medium heat, so that the bottom of the pan is well covered with oil. When hot enough to make crepes, dip an apple ring in the batter, lift it out with a fork, and let some of the excess batter drip off. Then transfer it to the frying pan. Repeat until the frying pan is full. The rings shouldn't touch each other.

Fry on one side for about 4 minutes, until golden brown and crisp, then turn the rings over and repeat on the other side.

Serve hot, with a sprinkling of cinnamon sugar.

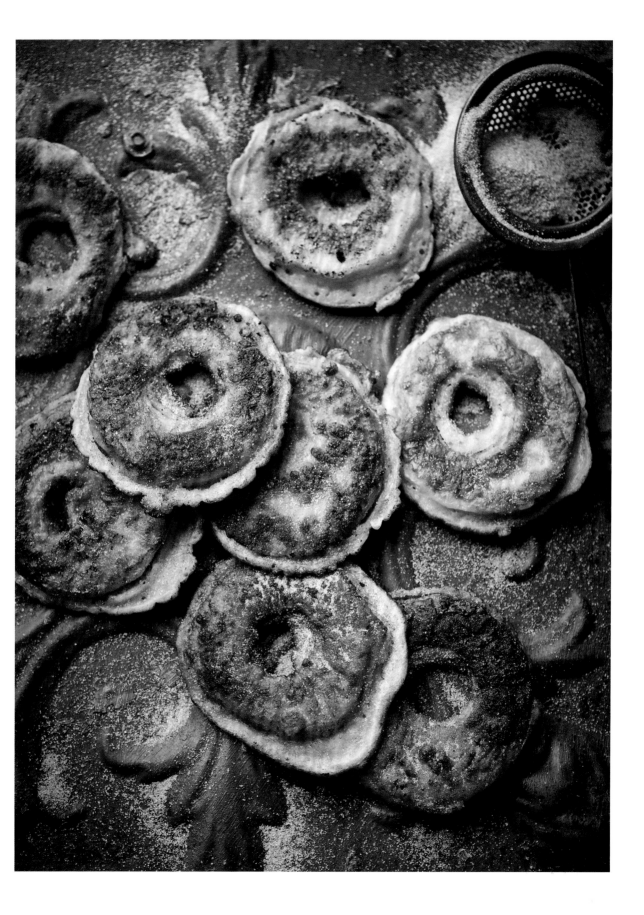

Striebele
Funnel Cake

These fried treats have many names—Striebele, Strauben, Trichterkuchen, funnel cake (in the US)—and many regions claim them as their own specialty. The German southwest, where I am from, is one of these regions, and often in German cookbooks they are described as a specialty from Baden. But the idea of pouring batter into hot oil using a funnel seems to have been almost universal, as there are very similar sweet snacks like this in India (jalebi) and the Arab world (e.g., zalabia in Algeria and Egypt).

One early childhood memory is of my grandma making them. In her kitchen there was a wood-fired range, and to deep-fry she removed some iron rings from the cooking surface. She had a deep-frying pot that could be inserted into this hole. It sealed off the gaps neatly so that fire and smoke couldn't escape, and the lower part of the pot was immersed in the flames. I always loved those crisp, fragile, irregular treats she made.

makes 6–8

YOU WILL NEED A FUNNEL AND A DEEP-FRYER
OR A DEEP FRYING PAN

3¼ CUPS (400G) ALL-PURPOSE FLOUR

1 PINCH SALT

1½ TABLESPOONS SUPERFINE SUGAR

1½ CUPS (350ML) WHOLE MILK

4 MEDIUM EGGS

1 TEASPOON VANILLA BEAN PASTE

2 TABLESPOONS UNSALTED BUTTER, MELTED

VEGETABLE OIL FOR DEEP-FRYING

CONFECTIONERS' SUGAR FOR DUSTING

Sift the flour, salt, and sugar into a bowl. Add the milk, eggs, and vanilla bean paste. Beat until you have a smooth batter. Add the melted butter and stir in.

Heat enough oil for deep-frying, in a deep, heavy pan or deep-fryer, making sure it is no more than half full, to about 350°F (180°C). You can tell that the oil is the correct temperature when air bubbles emerge immediately when dipping a wooden spoon in the oil.

Once the oil is hot, hold the funnel in one hand, with a finger sealing the tip. Ladle 2 to 3 tablespoons into the funnel. Now hold the funnel over the oil and release the finger. Move the funnel in irregular spiral movements to create a lattice of strands that hold together a bit.

Once the underside is light golden, turn over your funnel cake and fry until completely golden. This will take about 1–2 minutes.

Transfer the funnel cake onto paper towels to let the oil drip off. Repeat with the remaining batter. Serve sprinkled with confectioners' sugar.

Schoko-Waffeln
Chocolate Waffles

This variation of waffles uses melted chocolate as well as cocoa powder to get a rich chocolate flavor. They were a special treat in our family, and just need a light dusting of confectioners' sugar or a dollop of whipped cream to go with them.

makes about 10, depending on the size of your waffle maker

2 CUPS (245G) ALL-PURPOSE FLOUR

⅓ CUP (30G) COCOA POWDER

½ TEASPOON BAKING POWDER

1¾ OZ (50G) CHOCOLATE
(54% or 70% cocoa solids, to taste)

9 TABLESPOONS (125G) UNSALTED BUTTER,
CUBED, ROOM TEMPERATURE

1 PINCH SALT

⅓ CUP (75G) SUPERFINE SUGAR

3 MEDIUM EGGS, SEPARATED

1 TEASPOON VANILLA BEAN PASTE

1 CUP (225ML) WHOLE MILK,
ROOM TEMPERATURE

6 TABLESPOONS (100ML) SPARKLING WATER

CONFECTIONERS' SUGAR, FOR TOPPING

WHIPPED CREAM, TO SERVE

Sift the flour, cocoa powder, and baking powder into a bowl and set aside.

Melt the chocolate over a double boiler. To do this, place the chocolate in a heatproof bowl. Take a saucepan with a smaller diameter than the bowl and add about 1in (3cm) of boiling water. Place the bowl with chocolate on the saucepan, making sure the water does not touch the bowl. Stir from time to time. This melts the chocolate slowly.

Put the butter, salt, and sugar into a big bowl. Using a hand mixer or the balloon whisk on a stand mixer, beat until the mixture turns fluffy and changes color. Beat the egg yolks and vanilla bean paste into the butter mixture. Add the milk, flour mixture, and sparkling water bit by bit, alternating among the three.

Beat the egg whites to soft peaks. Fold the egg whites into the batter.

Fold the melted chocolate into the batter.

This waffle batter is best used immediately. The cooking time depends on the waffle maker used, but the waffles should be a bit crisp.

Serve with confectioners' sugar or a dollop of whipped cream.

Griess-Schnitten
Semolina Fritters

These have always been a favorite of my brother. My mother would have prepared the loaf of dough while we were at school, and she was ready when we came home at 1 p.m., exhausted and hungry, to feed us this treat.

The fritters are not very sweet, and the texture can be a bit unusual, but sprinkled with cinnamon sugar and served with apple sauce I am sure you will love them.

The semolina dough can be prepared well in advance.

Line a 1lb (500g) loaf pan, about 6 x 4in (15 x 9cm) with parchment paper or plastic wrap and set aside. This will help create nice rectangular slices.

Place the milk, butter, salt, nutmeg, and sugar in a saucepan and bring to a boil. Stir in the semolina and keep stirring until a lump forms. Take the saucepan off the heat and stir in one of the eggs. Transfer the semolina dough to the loaf pan, cover with plastic wrap or parchment paper and set aside to let it cool completely. The dough will set firm.

When you are ready to cook your fritters, beat the remaining egg and pour it onto a big plate. Spread the bread crumbs onto a second plate.

Remove the semolina block from the loaf pan and wrapping and cut it into ½in (1cm) thick slices.

Heat enough oil to coat the bottom of a frying pan on medium heat.

Take the semolina fritters one by one, coat them first in egg, then in bread crumbs, and fry them immediately until deep golden on each side, but not burned. This should take about 4 minutes per side.

Serve them hot, sprinkled with cinnamon sugar, and with apple sauce on the side. Summer fruit or plum compote goes well, too, and for a more luxurious dessert, why not serve them with a scoop of ice cream?

serves 4 as a dessert

2 CUPS (500ML) WHOLE MILK

1½ TABLESPOONS UNSALTED BUTTER

1 PINCH SALT

¼ TEASPOON GROUND NUTMEG

3 TABLESPOONS SUPERFINE SUGAR

¾ CUP (125G) FINE SEMOLINA

2 MEDIUM EGGS

BREAD CRUMBS, AS NEEDED

VEGETABLE OIL FOR FRYING

CINNAMON SUGAR (page 181) TO SERVE

APPLE SAUCE (page 181) TO SERVE

Oma's Waffeln
Grandma's Waffles

Waffles were always a treat, and often we would have them on Saturday evenings. Supper on Saturdays used to be quite early, because we had to catch Star Trek on TV, which aired at 6:10 p.m.! We sat around the table, the electric waffle maker in the middle, and the waffles were eaten as soon as they were ready.

Sift the flour and baking powder into a bowl and set aside.

Put the butter, salt, and sugar into a big bowl. Using a hand mixer or the balloon whisk on a stand mixer, beat together until it turns fluffy and changes color. Beat the egg yolks and vanilla bean paste into the butter mixture. Add the milk, flour mixture, and sparkling water bit by bit, alternating among the three.

Beat the egg whites to soft peaks. Fold the egg whites into the batter.

This waffle batter is best used immediately. The cooking time depends on the waffle maker used, but the waffles should be a bit crisp and a light golden color when ready.

Serve with confectioners' sugar, cinnamon sugar, or apple sauce.

makes about 12, depending on the size of your waffle maker

2⅔ CUPS (330G) ALL-PURPOSE FLOUR

½ TEASPOON BAKING POWDER

⅔ CUP (150G) UNSALTED BUTTER, CUBED, ROOM TEMPERATURE

1 PINCH SALT

½ CUP (100G) SUPERFINE SUGAR

4 MEDIUM EGGS, SEPARATED

1 TEASPOON VANILLA BEAN PASTE

1⅓ CUPS (330ML), ROOM TEMPERATURE

⅔ CUP (160ML) SPARKLING WATER

FOR TOPPING
CONFECTIONERS' SUGAR,
CINNAMON SUGAR (page 181),
OR APPLE SAUCE (page 181)

Dampfnudeln
Sweet Dumplings Steamed in Milk

You need a deep frying pan or a saucepan 8in (20cm) in diameter with a tight-fitting lid for these. If your lid has venting holes or lets out steam, it is important to cover those areas with a damp dish towel.

makes 4
in an 8in (20cm) pan

4 TABLESPOONS (60G) UNSALTED BUTTER,
ROOM TEMPERATURE

½ CUP (125ML) WHOLE MILK,
PLUS EXTRA FOR COOKING

2 CUPS (250G) BREAD FLOUR

3 TABLESPOONS SUPERFINE SUGAR,
PLUS EXTRA FOR SPRINKLING

1 PINCH SALT

1 TEASPOON INSTANT YEAST

1 MEDIUM EGG

Combine 2 tablespoons of the butter and the milk in a saucepan or bowl, and heat on the stove or in the microwave until lukewarm.

Combine the flour, 1½ tablespoons of the sugar, the salt, and yeast in a bowl. Pour in the milk and butter, add the egg and knead using your hands or a stand mixer fitted with a dough hook until a smooth ball forms. Cover and leave to proof in a warm place until well risen (use the poke test on page 197 to check if it's ready). Divide the dough into four equal pieces and shape them into balls. Cover them with a plastic bag or a dish towel and leave to proof for 30 minutes.

Meanwhile, add enough milk to cover the bottom of your pan or saucepan to a ½in (1cm) depth, plus the remaining butter and sugar.

When the dumplings have risen, bring the milk mixture to a boil, then reduce the heat so that the mixture simmers. Pour a little bit of sugar into a bowl, dip the bottom of each dumpling into the sugar and place the dumpling in the milk. Once all the dumplings are in the pan, put on the lid and seal it, if necessary. Steam the dumplings for about 30 minutes. You must not open the lid, or the dumplings will shrink and become unpalatable. It is hard to judge when they are done—you will have to listen. At first, you will hear the water boiling. This will go on for most of the time. When the noise changes to more of a crackling sound, like frying, the water has evaporated, and the dumplings are done. Continue to fry for another minute or two. You should also notice a light caramel scent.

There is no way to judge this by eye, even with a glass lid. And it is normal to have a few mishaps before mastering the recipe. But it is incredibly rewarding to make and delicious to eat. Dampfnudeln are best served with vanilla custard or Weinschaum-Crème (page 183). Fruit compote and vanilla ice cream are also great companions.

Salzige Dampfnudeln
Dumplings
Steamed in Salt Water

This recipe is simpler than the dumplings steamed in milk (opposite), and it is probably more widespread in Germany. Using less sugar and a brine for steaming means that these dumplings are equally suited to accompany a savory meal, such as goulash, or as a dessert with custard or wine sauce.

Combine the butter and milk in a saucepan or bowl, and heat on the stovetop or in the microwave until lukewarm. The butter needs to be lukewarm as well.

Put the flour, salt, and yeast into a bowl and mix. Add the milk mixture and knead using your hands or a stand mixer fitted with a dough hook until a smooth ball forms.

Cover the dough and leave it to proof in a warm place for about 1 hour, until well risen. You can use the poke test (see page 197) to check if it's ready. Divide the dough into four equal pieces and shape them into balls. Cover them with a plastic bag or a dish towel and let them proof for about 30 minutes.

Meanwhile, add water to an 8in (20cm) diameter pan to a ½in (1cm) depth and add the oil and ½ teaspoon of salt. Bring the water and oil to the boil and turn down the heat so that it simmers. Transfer the dumplings to the pan with enough space to expand and cover with the lid. (This recipe needs a tightly-fitting lid.) Steam the dumplings for about 30 minutes. You must not open the lid, or the dumplings will shrink and become unpalatable. It is hard to judge when they are done—you will have to listen. At first, you will hear the water boiling. This will go on for most of the time. When the noise changes to more of a crackling sound, like frying, the water has evaporated and the dumplings are done. Continue to fry for another minute or two.

Serve hot with savory dishes, or with custard or fruit compote.

*makes 4
in an 8in (20cm) pan*

1 TABLESPOON UNSALTED BUTTER, ROOM TEMPERATURE

9OZ (250ML) WHOLE MILK

1¼ CUPS (150G) BREAD FLOUR

1 TEASPOON SALT, PLUS ½ TEASPOON FOR STEAMING

1 TEASPOON INSTANT YEAST

1 TABLESPOON VEGETABLE OIL

EARLY ON, I WAS FASCINATED BY MOTORS AND GEARS, AND I HAD TO SEE WHAT WAS GOING ON UNDER THE HOOD. THIS FASCINATION HAS CARRIED OVER INTO MY APPROACH TO BAKING AS WELL.

Sheet cakes

*T*here is no easier way to make cake for a large number of people than to make a sheet cake. They can be easily portioned into squares, and everybody gets pretty much the same amount of filling. In Germany, sheet cakes are very popular at church bazaars, village fetes, birthday parties, and the like, but you can also buy them at bakeries.

There are a huge number of sheet cake recipes, and one specific kind of sheet cake deserves special mention: streuselkuchen, or "crumble cake." The main difference between and American or English crumble and German streusel is the texture. Crumble is akin to bread crumbs, whereas streusel is chunkier. The streusel dough is also worked just that little bit longer, which means it holds together more. The resulting texture and flavor are surprisingly different.

Often, streuselkuchen has a yeasted base, but it can also be made with a shortbread-like pastry, or a sponge cake base. There are no limits when it comes to fillings—fruit or custard in any combination are all possible— plus finely ground nuts or cocoa can be added to the streusel, too.

If being baked as a sheet cake, streuselkuchen will have a yeasted base or a sponge cake base, and can be found almost everywhere in Germany, from street corner bakeries to posh cafés to village festivals. In its simplest form, it is just a yeasted base topped with streusel—something I ate a lot of during my time at university!

In this chapter, I have included options to use a yeasted base or a sponge cake base, but please feel free to experiment.

Einfacher Streuselkuchen
Simple Streusel Cake

This cake is the easiest streuselkuchen to make, as it requires no filling, and it is surprisingly satisfying. When taking a bite, you immediately experience the contrast between the crunchy, sweet streusel topping and the soft, flaky base. A simple, but divine match. It was one of my favorite takeout treats when strolling through the streets of Freiburg.

makes 20 slices

1 PORTION STREUSEL (page 192)

1 PORTION BASIC YEASTED SWEET DOUGH (page 194) OR RICH YEASTED SWEET DOUGH (page 195)

UNSALTED BUTTER FOR GREASING

Prepare the streusel as directed on page 192.

Prepare the yeasted base according to the recipe on page 190 or 191. After the first proof, roll out the dough to fit a 14 x 11in (35 x 28cm) baking pan.

Lightly butter the baking sheet and line it with the dough. Leave to rise at room temperature for 30 minutes. This is to allow the dough to relax into its shape in the baking pan.

Meanwhile, preheat the oven to 350°F (180°C)

Using a brush or spray bottle, moisten the surface of the yeasted base. Tap water is fine.

Sprinkle the streusel onto the yeasted base, making sure it is evenly distributed, then bake for about 30 minutes, until the streusel is light golden-brown—the edges will be a bit darker.

Leave to cool in the pan for 5 minutes, then remove the cake from the pan and place on a wire rack to cool completely. This is best eaten fresh, but can be frozen or kept in an airtight container for up to 3 days.

Streuselkuchen mit Obst
Crumble Cake
with Apples, Rhubarb,
or Summer Fruit

This cake combines custard (or in German, Pudding) and fruit, so is essentially a crumble that you can eat with your hands.

Prepare the streusel as directed on page 188. Prepare the Vanilla Pudding as directed on page 184.

If using a yeasted base, prepare the yeasted base as directed on page 194 or 195. After the first proof, roll it out to fit a 14 x 11in (35 x 28cm) baking pan.

Lightly butter the baking pan and line it with the dough. Leave to rise at room temperature for 30 minutes. This is to allow the dough to relax into its shape in the baking pan. If using a basic sponge cake, spread the batter evenly in the baking pan.

Meanwhile, preheat the oven to 350°F (180°C).

Place all the fruit in a bowl and mix with the sugar.

Once the base is ready, spread the base with a layer of Vanilla Pudding, followed by a layer of the fruit, distributing it evenly. Lightly press the fruit into the pudding, then sprinkle the streusel on top, making sure that it, too, is evenly distributed.

If using a yeasted base, bake for about 30 minutes, until the streusel is light golden-brown—the edge of the yeasted base will be a bit darker. If using the basic sponge cake base, bake for about 50 minutes.

Leave to cool in the pan for 5 minutes, then remove the cake from the pan and place on a wire rack to cool completely. This is best eaten fresh, but can be frozen or kept in an airtight container for up to 3 days.

makes 20 slices

1 PORTION STREUSEL (page 192)

1 PORTION VANILLA PUDDING WITH EGG
(page 185)

1 PORTION OF
BASIC YEASTED SWEET DOUGH (page 194)
OR RICH YEASTED SWEET DOUGH (page 195)
OR BASIC SPONGE CAKE (page 192)

UNSALTED BUTTER FOR GREASING

2 APPLES, PEELED, CORED, AND CUBED
(use apples that stay firm when cooked,
e.g., Granny Smith)

10½OZ (300G) RHUBARB, TRIMMED AND CUT INTO
½IN (1CM) PIECES, OR SUMMER FRUIT (frozen)

2 TABLESPOONS SUPERFINE SUGAR

makes 25 slices

FOR THE CAKE
1½ CUPS (350G) UNSALTED BUTTER,
ROOM TEMPERATURE

1⅔ CUPS (270G) SUPERFINE SUGAR

7 MEDIUM EGGS,
ROOM TEMPERATURE

3⅔ CUPS (450G) ALL-PURPOSE FLOUR

1 TABLESPOON BAKING POWDER

½ CUP (50G) COCOA POWDER

2 X 14OZ (400G) JARS MORELLO CHERRIES
IN SYRUP
(or similar, pitted cherries)

FOR THE BUTTERCREAM
1 PORTION VANILLA PUDDING
(page 184)

1 CUP + 2 TABLESPOONS (250G) UNSALTED
BUTTER, CUBED,
ROOM TEMPERATURE

⅔ CUP (80G) CONFECTIONERS' SUGAR, UNSIFTED

FOR THE GLAZE
12OZ (350G) DARK CHOCOLATE
(70% cocoa solids), BROKEN INTO PIECES

2 TABLESPOONS COCONUT OIL
OR UNSALTED BUTTER

Donauwellen
(The Waves of the Danube)

This cake is a real classic. The source of the Danube is in the Black Forest, so it is no surprise that the flavors are very similar to Black Forest gateau. But Donauwellen looks very different, and no alcohol is involved. When the cake is assembled, you just see a flat piece of chocolate from above. Cut into it and the waves are revealed: during baking, the cherries sink into the layers of chocolate sponge cake and plain sponge cake beneath to create the wave pattern. The cake is topped with a vanilla buttercream and glazed with chocolate. The amounts given are for a large, deep baking pan.

Preheat the oven to 350°F (180°C).

To prepare the batter, make sure the ingredients are at room temperature. If the eggs and butter are too cold, the mix might split when combined.

Put the butter and 1 cup + 2 tablespoons (220g) of the sugar in a bowl and beat, using a hand mixer or a stand mixer fitted with the balloon whisk, until frothy and light. Add the eggs one by one while continuing to beat, waiting for each egg to be incorporated well before adding the next.

Sift the flour and baking powder together. Mix this into the butter and eggs bit by bit.

Line a large, deep baking pan, approximately 12 x 16in (30 x 40cm) and 1½in (3cm) deep with parchment paper and spread half of the batter evenly onto it. For the chocolate batter, mix together the cocoa powder and remaining sugar and sift it into the bowl with the plain batter. Mix well until the batter is smooth. Spread the chocolate batter evenly on top of the plain batter, trying not to disturb the plain batter underneath.

Place the cherries on top of the chocolate batter, about 1½in (3cm) from each other, and very slightly push them into the batter.

Bake on the center rack of the oven about 25 minutes; a skewer inserted into the center of the cake should come out clean. Leave to cool in the pan.

For the buttercream, prepare the vanilla pudding as directed on page 184. Beat the butter with the confectioners' sugar until it is very frothy and light. While the vanilla pudding is still lukewarm, beat it into the butter bit by bit.

Once the cake is cool, spread the buttercream evenly on top.

For the chocolate glaze, put the chocolate into a heatproof bowl, together with the oil, and melt over a double boiler, or in a microwave. Be careful not to overheat the chocolate. Once it is melted, let it cool down to about about 85°F (30°C), stirring gently without incorporating any air. Spread the chocolate glaze evenly on top of the buttercream.

Put the cake in a cool place and let the chocolate glaze set.

Trim the edges and cut into portion-sized rectangles to serve. This cake keeps for at least 3 days in an airtight container, longer in the fridge.

Butterkuchen
Butter Cake

This cake is very popular because it's so easy to make, plus it's an ideal way to show off your fluffy yeasted base.

makes 20 slices

1 PORTION BASIC YEASTED SWEET DOUGH
OR RICH YEASTED SWEET DOUGH
(page 194 or page 195)

⅔ CUP (150G) UNSALTED BUTTER, COLD, CUBED,
PLUS EXTRA FOR GREASING

HEAPING ¾ CUP (150G) SUPERFINE SUGAR

1 CUP (100G) SLIVERED ALMONDS

Line a 14 x 11in (35 x 28cm) baking pan with parchment paper.

Prepare the yeasted base as directed on page 194 or 195. After the first proof, roll it out to fit the prepared baking pan.

Lightly butter the baking pan and line it with the dough. Leave to rise at room temperature for 30 minutes. This is to allow the dough to relax into its shape in the baking pan.

Push the butter cubes into the dough, about one every 2½in (4cm), and sprinkle with the sugar and almonds. Allow to rise for a further 15 minutes.

Meanwhile, preheat the oven to 350°F (180°C).

Bake for 25–30 minutes, until your cake has a beautiful golden color. Take care not to burn the almonds. Watch the oven temperature, as many ovens are hotter than the setting. If the yeast base needs more time, cover the cake with foil and continue baking, checking every 5 minutes.

This cake can be eaten slightly warm. It is best eaten fresh, but can be kept for a couple of days in an airtight container, or portions can be frozen.

Pudding Streuselkuchen
Custard Crumble Cake

Custard (or in German, Pudding) is another very popular choice for a streuselkuchen filling, and it is my personal favorite. The thickness of the custard layer may vary according to the taste of the baker. My choice would be to have enough custard so that it shows up as a distinct layer, rather than a thin spread, but anything is possible and tasty.

makes 20 slices

1 PORTION STREUSEL
(page 192)

1 PORTION VANILLA PUDDING WITH EGG
(page 185)

1 PORTION OF
BASIC YEASTED SWEET DOUGH (page 194) OR
RICH YEASTED SWEET DOUGH (page 195) OR
BASIC SPONGE CAKE CAKEE BASE (page 192)

UNSALTED BUTTER FOR GREASING

Prepare the streusel as directed on page 192.

Prepare the vanilla pudding as directed on page 184.

Prepare the yeasted base as directed on page 194 or 195. After the first proof, roll it out to fit a 14 x 11in (35 x 28cm) baking pan.

Lightly butter the baking pan and line it with the dough. Leave to rise at room temperature for 30 minutes. This is to allow the dough to relax into its shape in the baking pan.

If using a basic 350°F (180°C), spread the batter evenly in the baking pan.

Meanwhile, preheat the oven to 350°F (180°C).

Once the base is ready, spread the pudding evenly over the top. The thickness of the pudding layer is down to personal taste, but the amounts given work well for me. Sprinkle the streusel on top, making sure it's evenly distributed.

If using a yeasted base, bake for about 30 minutes, until the streusel is light golden-brown—the edge of the yeasted base will be a bit darker. If using the basic sponge cake base, bake for about 50 minutes.

Leave to cool in the pan for 5 minutes, then remove the cake from the pan and place on a wire rack to cool completely. This is best eaten fresh, but can be frozen or kept in an airtight container for up to 3 days.

Apfel-Streuselkuchen
Apple Crumble Cake

Just adding apple cubes to a simple streuselkuchen creates a very different cake. The apples introduce moistness, acidity, and a third texture, creating a slice of cake that can be quite refreshing on a warm July day at a village fair.

Prepare the streusel as directed on page 192.

If using a yeasted base, prepare the yeasted base according to the recipe on page 194 or 195. After the first proof, roll it out to fit a 14 x 11in (35 x 28cm) baking pan.

Lightly butter the baking pan and line it with the dough. Leave to rise at room temperature for 30 minutes. This is to allow the dough to relax into its shape in the baking pan.

If using a basic sponge cake, spread the batter evenly in the baking pan.

Meanwhile, preheat the oven to 350°F (180°C).

Place the apples in a bowl, add the sugar and spices, and mix well. Once the dough is ready, distribute the apples evenly over the surface and lightly press them down. Sprinkle the streusel on top, making sure it's evenly distributed.

If using a yeasted base, bake for about 30 minutes, until the streusel is light golden-brown—the edge of the yeasted base will be a bit darker. If using the basic sponge cake base, bake for about 50 minutes.

Leave to cool in the pan for 5 minutes, then remove the cake from the pan and place on a wire rack to cool completely. This is best eaten fresh, but can be frozen or kept in an airtight container for up to 3 days.

makes 20 slices

1 PORTION STREUSEL (page 192)

1 PORTION OF
BASIC YEASTED SWEET DOUGH (page 194) OR
RICH YEASTED SWEET DOUGH (page 195) OR
BASIC SPONGE CAKE BASE (page 192)

UNSALTED BUTTER FOR GREASING

5 FIRM, SLIGHTLY TART APPLES, PEELED,
CORED, AND CUBED

2 TABLESPOONS SUPERFINE SUGAR

1 TEASPOON GROUND CINNAMON

½ TEASPOON GROUND CORIANDER

Schoko-Streuselkuchen mit Birne
Chocolate Pear Crumble Cake

A variation on the Birne Helene (pear Helene) theme. A teaspoon of ground cardamom is added to the base, and ¼ cup (25g) of the flour in the streusel is replaced with cocoa powder.

makes 20 slices

1 PORTION STREUSEL (page 192),
BUT SUBSTITUTE ¼ CUP (25G) FLOUR WITH
¼ CUP (25G) COCOA POWDER

1 PORTION OF
BASIC YEASTED SWEET DOUGH (page 194) OR
RICH YEASTED SWEET DOUGH (page 195) OR
BASIC SPONGE CAKE BASE (page 192)
WITH 1 TEASPOON GROUND CARDAMOM
ADDED TO THE FLOUR

UNSALTED BUTTER FOR GREASING

4 FIRM PEARS, SUCH AS CONFERENCE
PEELED, CORED, AND CUBED

2 TABLESPOONS SUPERFINE SUGAR

Prepare the streusel as directed on page 192, substituting ¼ cup (25g) of the flour with ¼ cup (25g) cocoa powder.

If using a yeasted base, prepare the yeasted base as directed on page 194 or 195, adding the cardamom to the flour. After the first proof, roll it out to fit a 14 x 11in (35 x 28cm) baking pan.

Lightly butter the baking pan and line it with the dough. Leave to rise at room temperature for 30 minutes. This is to allow the dough to relax into its shape in the baking pan.

If using a basic sponge cake, spread the batter evenly in the baking pan.

Meanwhile, preheat the oven to 350°F (180°C).

Place the pears in a bowl and mix with the sugar.

Once the base is ready, spread evenly with the pieces of pear, lightly pressing them into the dough, then sprinkle the streusel on top, making sure it, too, is evenly distributed.

If using a yeasted base, bake for about 30 minutes, until the edge of the yeasted base is a medium golden-brown. If using the basic sponge cake base, bake for about 50 minutes.

Leave to cool in the pan for 5 minutes, then remove the cake from the pan and place on a wire rack to cool completely. This is best eaten fresh, but can be frozen or kept in an airtight container for up to 3 days.

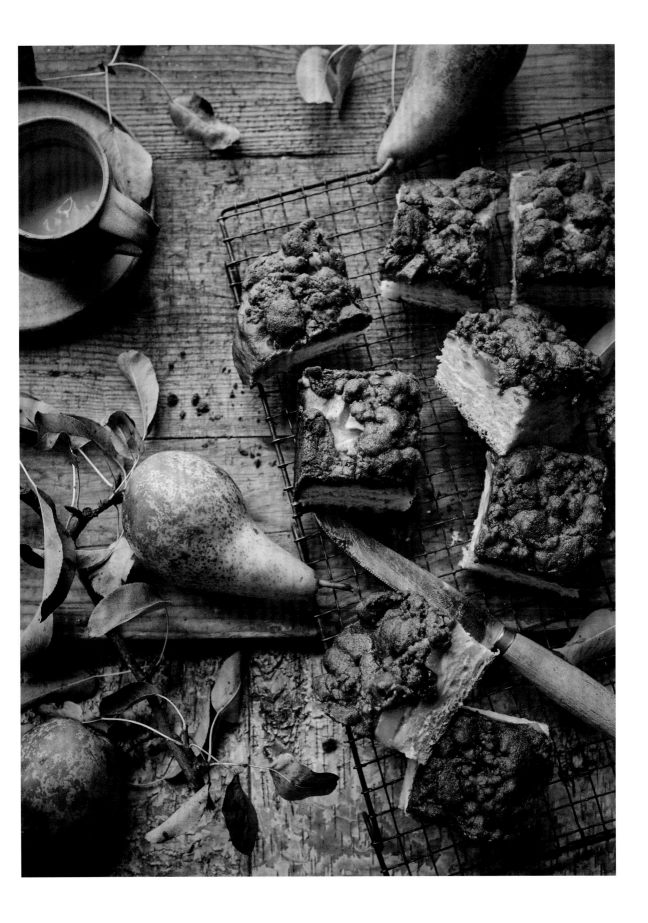

Schoko-Apfel-Streuselkuchen
Chocolate Apple Crumble Cake

This streuselkuchen variation is for the chocolate addicts. The soft, moist, acidic apple pieces and the sweet, rich chocolate custard are a great match, sandwiched between crisp streusel and a flaky base, every bite is a an adventure. This cake is my family's favorite streuselkuchen.

makes 20 slices

1 PORTION
BASIC YEASTED SWEET DOUGH (page 194) OR
RICH YEASTED SWEET DOUGH (page 195) OR
BASIC SPONGE CAKE BASE (page 192)

1 PORTION STREUSEL
(page 192)

1 PORTION VANILLA PUDDING WITH EGG
(page 185)

3½OZ (100G) DARK CHOCOLATE
(70% cocoa solids), BROKEN INTO PIECES

UNSALTED BUTTER FOR GREASING

5 FIRM, SLIGHTLY TART APPLES, SUCH AS
GRANNY SMITH, PEELED, CORED, AND CUBED

2 TABLESPOONS SUPERFINE SUGAR

½ TEASPOON GROUND CLOVES

Prepare the yeasted base as directed on page 194 or 195. Prepare the streusel as directed on page 192. Prepare the vanilla custard as directed on page 185 and allow to cool. Melt the chocolate either in a microwave or in a bowl set over a pan of simmering water (but don't allow the bowl to touch the water). Make sure the chocolate is just liquid; overheating will break the chocolate and render it unusable.

Once the custard has cooled, stir in the melted chocolate.

If using a yeasted base, after the base has had its first proof, roll it out to fit a 14 x 11in (35 x 28cm) baking pan.

Lightly butter the baking pan and line it with the dough. Leave to rise at room temperature for 30 minutes. This is to allow the dough to relax into its shape in the baking pan. If using a basic sponge cake, spread the batter evenly in the baking pan.

Meanwhile, preheat the oven to 350°F (180°C). Place the apples in a bowl, add the sugar and ground cloves, and mix well.

Spread a layer of the chocolate pudding evenly over the base. Distribute the apples evenly over the top, lightly push them down into the custard, then sprinkle with the streusel, making sure that it, too, is evenly distributed.

If using a yeasted base, bake for about 30 minutes, until the streusel is light golden-brown—the edge of the yeasted base will be a bit darker. If using the basic sponge cake base, bake for about 50 minutes.

Leave to cool in the pan for 5 minutes, then remove from the pan and place on a wire rack to cool completely. This is best eaten fresh, but can be frozen or kept in an airtight container for up to 3 days

THE HOUSE WHERE I GREW UP. THIS PHOTO IS FROM AROUND 1950.

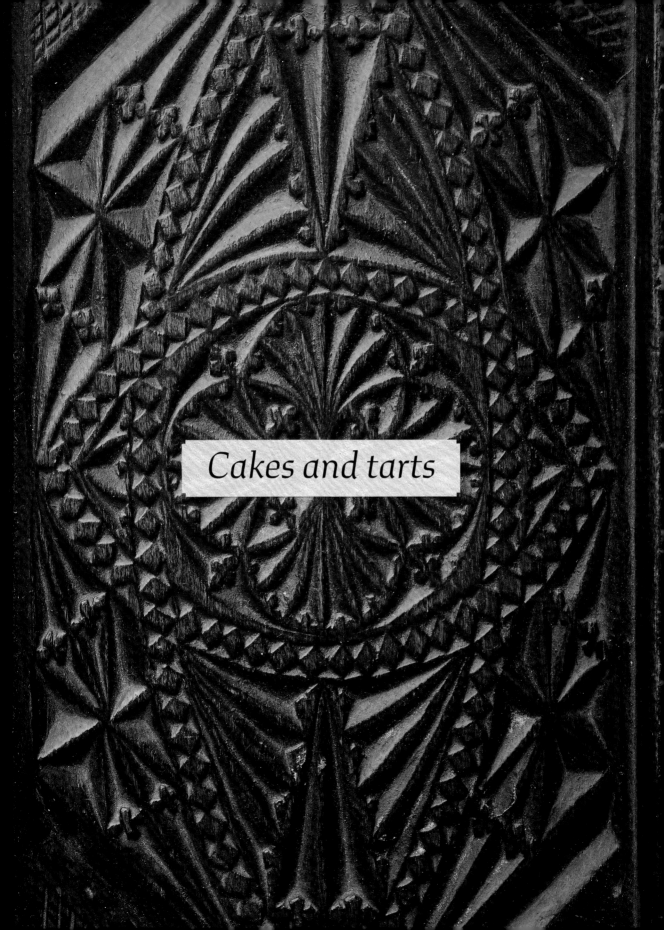

Cakes and tarts

*T*he village where I grew up is on the outskirts of Freiburg. Perched above a long valley, even today, it still feels remote from the city. On the many occasions when we went into town by public transportation, we had to walk a little way to catch the bus, then change to the trolley, which would eventually arrive right in the center of Freiburg. During the journey, the scenery outside changed. Starting out with views of forest, meadows, and cows, as the journey progressed, the houses got bigger and less familiar, and I knew we would arrive soon when the trolley crossed the Dreisam River and then passed through an old gate with murals of St. George.

This change of scenery, and the smells, sounds, and unfamiliar movements of bus and trolley was a great prelude for the two things I always looked forward to most: the toy shops and the cake buffet in the department stores. Those department stores changed a lot over time, and the victims of the change in the Eighties were the huge cafés on their top floors, whose space was repurposed for selling camping equipment.

The views of the cathedral and market square from those rooftop cafés were stunning. The furniture was wooden, solid and durable, and a fleet of waitresses served the huge crowd that regularly gathered every afternoon to have their coffee and cake. The cake buffet was gigantic, in my memory. I had my favorite cake—the Black Forest gateau—but I was always attracted to the very neat mousse cakes and Charlottes.

The store's bakers seemed to have an endless repertoire of interior and exterior cake designs.

It is very fitting that my son Benjamin's choice of birthday cake from early on was a fruit Charlotte; he asked for one for his eighth birthday, and this wish led to a great boost for my baking!

In terms of tarts, Linzer Torte has a very special place in our family. My mother used to make it all year round, with the help of my brother and me. But for Advent and Christmas, we always made several Linzer tarts at a time to store them, as they improve a lot over time. They were then a coffee-table staple on Christmas Day and Boxing Day, when relatives came round for a visit.

For our wedding, Sophia and I asked my mother to make Linzer Torte as a treat after the ceremony, which she happily did. All our guests had walked a long way through wind and rain to the cliffs of the Seven Sisters. During the service, the clouds broke, and we were blessed with sunshine in that most beautiful scenery. After the ceremony, we served my mother's Linzer Torte, which she brought all the way from Germany, along with special wine from Freiburg. Then we headed off to the top of the cliffs, to have a dance while the Klezmer band played.

All the following cakes would not have been out of place in one of the department store cafés of my childhood.

Schwarzwälder Kirschtorte
Black Forest Gateau

serves 12

FOR THE CHERRY FILLING
1LB (450G) MORELLO CHERRIES
OR BLACK CHERRIES IN SYRUP (drained), PITTED

¼ CUP (60ML) KIRSCH

9OZ (250ML) SYRUP FROM CHERRIES

⅓ CUP (40G) CORNSTARCH

2 TABLESPOONS WATER

HEAPING ½ CUP (120G) SUPERFINE SUGAR

FOR THE KIRSCH SYRUP
¼ CUP (60ML) WATER

¼ CUP (60G) SUPERFINE SUGAR

¼ CUP (60ML) KIRSCH

FOR THE PIE DOUGH
⅞ CUP (100G) ALL-PURPOSE FLOUR,
PLUS EXTRA FOR DUSTING

2 TABLESPOONS SUPERFINE SUGAR

5½ TABLESPOONS (80G)
UNSALTED BUTTER, CUBED

1 TABLESPOON BEATEN EGG

½ TEASPOON VANILLA BEAN PASTE

APRICOT JAM, TO COVER PIE CRUST BOTTOM

As every viewer of The Great British Bake Off *knows, this is my personal favorite. It is the measure by which I would judge a café or a bakery. The balance among cream, kirsch, and chocolate needs to be just right. Shortcuts don't work, and I would be very reluctant to change this flavor profile into something novel. Not every pâtissier adds a pie dough bottom, but I find that a little crunch makes an otherwise very soft texture far more interesting. Morello cherries are preferred, but black cherries in light syrup are okay, although not as flavorful.*

Don't be intimidated by the long list of ingredients and steps— each single step is quite easy, and the outcome will be rewarding, I promise. Many of the components can be prepared the day before the cake is needed: pie dough crust, sponge cakes, cherry filling, and kirsch syrup. With those things in place, assembly is very quick.

For the cherry filling, soak the drained cherries in the kirsch overnight. Drain the cherries and reserve the kirsch. Put the kirsch into a measuring cup and add enough of the reserved syrup to get 1¼ cups (300ml) of liquid.

Dissolve the cornstarch in the water and add to the kirsch mixture in a saucepan. Add the sugar and carefully bring to a boil while stirring. Once the liquid has boiled and thickened, and no longer tastes of starch, take it off the heat and carefully stir in the cherries. Set aside and leave to cool completely.

For the kirsch syrup, combine the water and sugar in a small saucepan and bring to a boil while stirring. Once the sugar has dissolved completely, take it off the heat and leave to cool completely. Add the kirsch.

To make the pie dough, put all the ingredients in a bowl and mix with your hands until the dough is smooth. Wrap in plastic wrap and set aside in the fridge for about 30 minutes, until the dough is just firm enough to roll out.

Preheat the oven to 350°F (180°C). Lightly grease a 10in (25cm) springform or sandwich pan.

continued

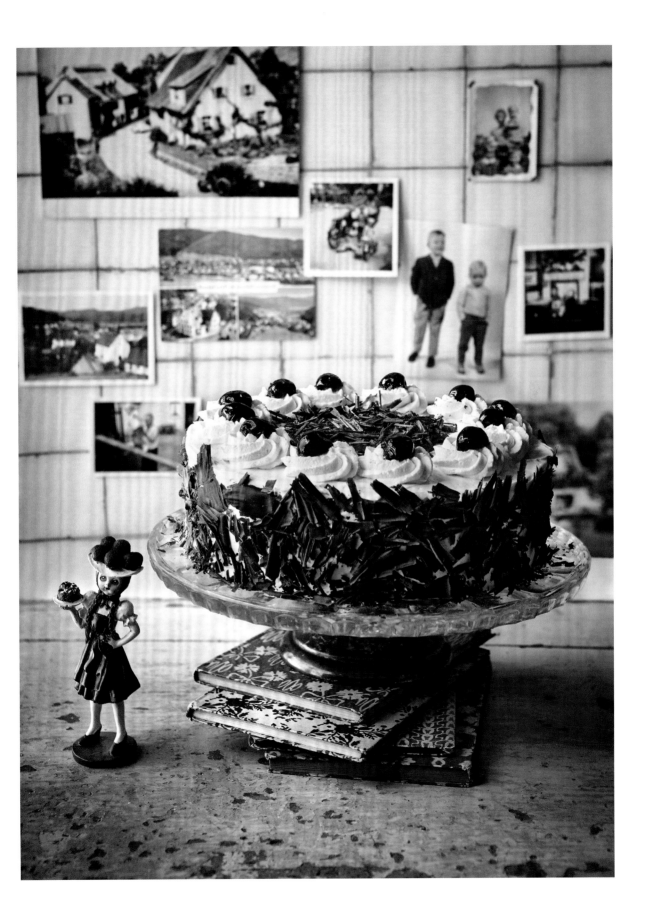

FOR THE CHOCOLATE SPONGE CAKE
6 MEDIUM EGGS

⅞ CUP (160G) SUPERFINE SUGAR

½ TEASPOON SALT

¾ CUP (90G) ALL-PURPOSE FLOUR

½ CUP (55G) CORNSTARCH

⅓ CUP (30G) COCOA POWDER

3 TABLESPOONS UNSALTED BUTTER,
MELTED, PLUS EXTRA FOR GREASING

FOR THE CREAM FILLING
17OZ (500ML) HEAVY CREAM

1OZ (30ML) KIRSCH

⅓ CUP +1 TABLESPOON (40G)
CONFECTIONERS' SUGAR, SIFTED

TO FINISH
1¼ CUPS (300ML) HEAVY CREAM

2 TABLESPOONS CONFECTIONERS' SUGAR, SIFTED

6 CANDIED CHERRIES, HALVED

CHOCOLATE SHAVINGS, AS NEEDED

On a floured surface, roll out the dough to a circle about ⅛in (3mm) thick. Transfer the dough to the prepared pan, cutting off any surplus as only the bottom of the pan needs to be covered. Prick the pie crust with a fork so that trapped air can escape during baking.

Bake for 8–10 minutes, until the edges start to brown.

For the chocolate sponge cake, lightly grease a 10in (25cm) springform cake pan and line the bottom with parchment paper. Increase the oven temperature to 425°F (220°C).

Sift the flour, cornstarch, and cocoa powder together into a bowl. Set aside.

Put some water in a saucepan and bring to a boil. This is for heating the bowl with the eggs.

Put the eggs, sugar, and salt in a bowl.

Place the bowl with the eggs over the simmering water and beat with a hand mixer on medium speed until the eggs reach a temperature of about 110°F (43°C). The bowl should not touch the water in the saucepan beneath.

Take the bowl off the boiling water and continue beating on high speed until the eggs are cold and have reached the ribbon stage, i.e., when the beater is pulled out of the mix and moved across the surface it creates a ribbon of egg froth that slowly disappears.

Fold the sifted flour mixture into the eggs, then stir the melted butter in to the mixture.

Pour the batter into the prepared pan and bake for about 15 minutes, until a skewer inserted into the center comes out clean. Leave to cool before taking out of the pan.

Cut the top off the cooled sponge cake to even it out, if necessary. Cut the sponge cake into three equal layers, reserving the most even layer for the top.

For the cream filling, combine the heavy cream, kirsch, and confectioners' sugar and whip to stiff peaks.

Place the pie crust on a cake board. Heat some apricot jam so that it is just liquid enough to be spread easily. Cover the pie crust with a thin layer of apricot jam.

Place the bottom sponge cake layer on top of the pie crust and brush with kirsch syrup.

Transfer some of the cream filling into a piping bag with a large round nozzle and pipe two concentric rings, starting at the edge, and a bullseye. Fill the gaps with cherry filling. It should be thick enough to hold its place. This should look like a target disk or dartboard with five zones, from the middle: cream—cherries—cream—cherries—cream.

Select your second sponge cake, turn it upside down and brush the underside with kirsch syrup. Place the sponge cake brushed-side down on top of the bottom sponge cake and filling.

Repeat the steps—brush the top of the sponge cakes—apply cream and cherry fillings—brush the bottom of third sponge cake and place it on top of the cake, syrup-side down. Gently press down the top sponge cake and even out any irregularities. If there is a bit of cream filling left, use it to apply a thin crumb layer.

To finish off the cake, beat the cream and confectioners' sugar to soft peaks. Don't overbeat or the mixture will set and break when piping. The starch in the confectioners' sugar will stabilize the whipped cream and help it keep its shape for longer.

Reserve enough of the whipped cream in a piping bag with a medium star nozzle to pipe 12 pirouettes (the classic decoration) and any other decorations you like. Cover the cake evenly with the remaining cream and smooth the surface. Pipe 12 pirouettes, one for each slice of cake, around the edge. Top each pirouette with half a candied cherry. Cover the sides and the center of the cake with chocolate shavings.

This cake will be good for 3 days. It needs to be kept in the fridge.

serves 12

FOR THE FILLING
7OZ (200ML) WHOLE MILK

1¾ CUPS (450ML) HEAVY CREAM

1 VANILLA POD

5 MEDIUM EGG YOLKS

⅓ CUP (60G) SUPERFINE SUGAR

¼ CUP (35G) CORNSTARCH

2 GELATIN SHEETS OR
½ TABLESPOON (½ ENVELOPE) GELATIN POWDER

ZEST OF 1 LEMON

2 TEASPOONS VANILLA BEAN PASTE

FOR THE YEASTED BASE
2¾ CUPS (340G) BREAD FLOUR

3 TABLESPOONS SUPERFINE SUGAR

1½ TEASPOONS INSTANT YEAST

½ TEASPOON SALT

¾ CUP (170ML) WHOLE MILK, LUKEWARM

1½ TABLESPOONS UNSALTED BUTTER,
ROOM TEMPERATURE,
PLUS EXTRA FOR GREASING

1 MEDIUM EGG YOLK

ZEST OF 1 LEMON

FOR THE TOPPING
5½ TABLESPOONS (80G) UNSALTED BUTTER

⅓ CUP (80G) SUPERFINE SUGAR

⅔ CUP (80G) SLIVERED ALMONDS FLAKED
ALMONDS

¼ CUP (50ML) HEAVY CREAM

2 TABLESPOONS HONEY

Bienenstich
Beesting Cake

Bienenstich is my mother's favorite, and an absolute classic. But the way it presents itself in cafés can be quite varied. The common elements are: a yeasted cake, topped with an almond sugar mixture, sliced into two layers, and filled with some sort of cream. No matter how it has been made, the huge difference in textures make it the messiest German cake to eat, but that is part of the fun!

The filling can be made the day before if you like. Pour the milk and 1¼cups (300ml) of the heavy cream cream into a saucepan. Split the vanilla pod and scrape out the seeds. Add the seeds to the milk and bring to scalding point. While the milk is heating up, place the egg yolks, sugar, and cornstarch in a bowl and beat until smooth.

Once the milk is hot, slowly pour one-third of it into the egg yolks while stirring. Pour this mixture back into the saucepan while stirring and return the saucepan to the heat. Slowly bring to a boil. When the milk starts boiling, quickly take the saucepan off the heat and pour the custard into a bowl. Take care not to overheat this custard: the starch prevents the egg yolk from coagulating, but the fat of the cream can separate from the mixture, which makes it unusable. Cover the surface with plastic wrap to prevent a skin from forming and set aside to cool.

To make the yeasted base, put all the ingredients in a bowl and, using your hands, mix and knead until a smooth ball forms. Continue kneading for another couple of minutes—a short knead is enough for this cake. Cover and leave to rest for 2 hours at room temperature.

Once the yeasted dough has proved, lightly grease a 10in (25cm) springform cake pan with butter.

Roll out the dough to a disk the size of the prepared pan—you don't need flour on the work surface—and transfer it into the pan. It should stretch all the way to the sides of the pan without creating a rim. Make sure you have an even thickness. Set aside.

To prepare the topping, put all the ingredients into a saucepan and heat over medium heat, stirring constantly until the mixture thickens. This can take a few minutes. It should be spreadable but not runny, and not caramelized. Once this consistency is reached, let the mixture cool a bit while stirring.

With a teaspoon, place little heaps of the warm topping on top of the base in the pan. Make sure they are equally distributed. Now, spread the topping to cover the base evenly, using a spatula or a pastry knife. This is an essential step: if the topping is uneven the cake will balloon at the thinner spots.

Let the cake rest for another 30 minutes. Because of the topping, you don't need to cover it.

Meanwhile, preheat the oven to 350°F (180°C).

continued

Bake in the lower third of the oven for about 25 minutes. The color should be a nice, medium golden-brown, like Florentines. Leave the cake to cool for 15 minutes, then carefully remove from the pan so you do not rip the topping apart. At this point, you can use a knife to mark the slices and even cut carefully through the topping—it will make it much easier to serve the cake later. Transfer to a wire rack and let cool completely.

The assembly should be done as close to eating as possible. To finish the filling, soak the gelatin sheets in cold water, if using, or add the gelatin powder. Add the lemon zest and vanilla bean paste to the custard and beat until it is smooth. Whisk the remaining heavy cream until it is moderately stiff.

Take the gelatin sheets out of the water and put them in a small pan. Heat them until they melt—this will be very quick. Add the liquid gelatin to the custard and whisk. Fold in the whipped cream.

Cut the cake horizontally. Remove the top—don't turn it upside down. Spread the filling on the bottom of the Bienenstich; it should be at least as thick as the bottom cake layer. A piping bag with a big round nozzle is very useful for this. Place the top of the Bienenstich on top of the filling and lightly squeeze down.

Let the cream set a little while—ideally, put the cake in the fridge for 20 minutes or so.

Bienenstich is best eaten fresh and needs to be kept cool.

serves 12

FOR THE SPONGE CAKES
6 MEDIUM EGGS, SEPARATED

⅞ CUP (175G) SUPERFINE SUGAR

¾ CUP (90G) ALL-PURPOSE FLOUR

¾ CUP (85G) CORNSTARCH

¼ CUP (60G) UNSALTED BUTTER, MELTED

FOR THE FILLING
9OZ (250G) MARZIPAN
(page 189 or ready-made)

3 TABLESPOONS WHISKEY

FOR THE GANACHE
5OZ (150G) CHOCOLATE
(54% cocoa solids),
BROKEN INTO PIECES

7OZ (200ML) HEAVY CREAM

Herren-Torte
Gentlemen's Cake

This cake with its many layers was one of the cakes that attracted me to those huge cake displays in department stores. There are several traditional cakes and desserts in Germany that contain the word Herren *in their name, the German word for gentlemen. It is always a hint that strong, unusual flavors are being used. The original Herren-Torte was invented in the 1930s and features thin sponge cakes alternating with wine-flavored marzipan, but in my recipe I am using whiskey.*

For the sponge cakes, prepare eight sheets of parchment paper. Using a pencil, draw a circle of 10in (25cm) diameter on each of the sheets of paper. Turn the paper upside down so that the batter won't come into contact with the pencil.

Preheat the oven to 425°F (220°C).

Divide the eggs whites and yolks between two big heatproof bowls. Pour half the sugar into the yolks. Beat the egg whites to soft peaks. Slowly add the remaining sugar bit by bit and whip to stiff peaks.

Sift the flour and cornstarch together.

Over a pan of boiling water, beat the sugar and egg yolks until they reach a temperature of about 110°F (43°C). Remove the bowl and continue beating until the egg yolks are pale, frothy, and creamy. Fold one-third of the egg white into the egg yolks. Then fold in the remaining egg white. Fold in the flour mixture, followed by the melted butter.

The batter is enough for eight sponge cakes. Depending on your equipment, you can bake up to three sponge cakes in one batch.

Spread the batter thinly inside the circles on the parchment paper. Transfer the parchment paper onto baking sheets and bake for 6–8 minutes. Don't overbake; the thin sponge cakes can dry

out very quickly and get brittle. Leave to cool and repeat the previous steps until you have baked all eight sponge cakes.

For the filling, knead the marzipan to soften it and break it into little pieces. Add the whiskey and stir until you have a smooth paste without any lumps.

To assemble the cake, make sure all eight sponge cakes are the same size. Trim them, if necessary. Place the bottom sponge cake on a cake plate and thinly cover with whiskey filling. Place the next sponge cake on top of the whiskey filling and coat thinly. Continue in this way until you have added all the sponge cakes. Use whiskey filling to cover the sides and the top of the cake—only a very thin layer is necessary to even out little irregularities.

For the ganache, break the chocolate into little pieces and put the pieces into a bowl. Pour the heavy cream into a pan and bring to scalding point. Pour the hot heavy cream over the chocolate and wait for about 2 minutes. Then stir the mixture using a whisk, but don't beat in any air bubbles.

Once the ganache is shiny, use it to coat the cake. Let the ganache set, then mark the cake slices with the back of a knife. For decoration, melt some chocolate and pipe the letter H (for Herren) on each slice. This cake improves in flavor over time and keeps very well in an airtight container for 3 days.

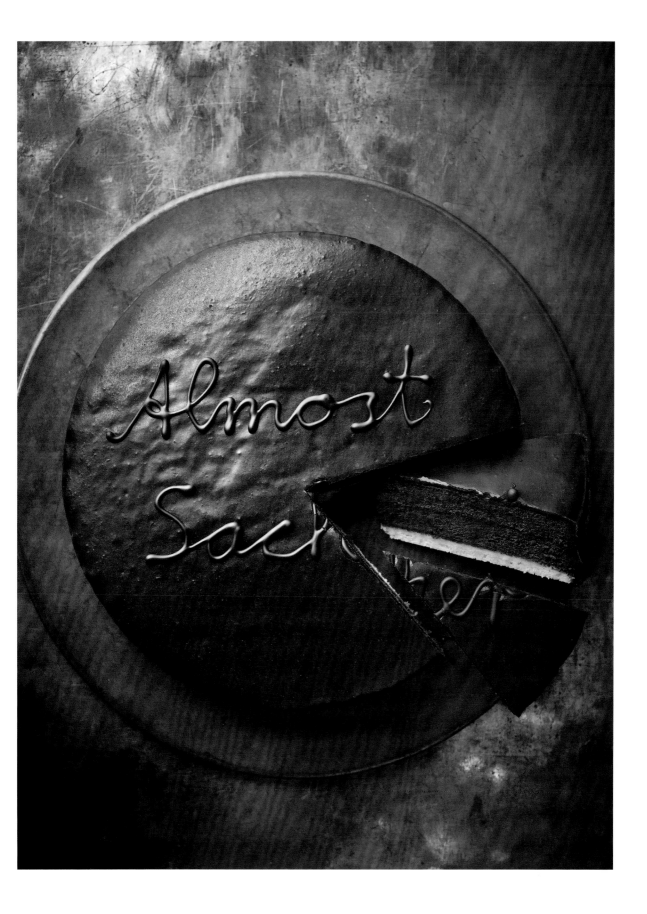

Almost Sacher Torte

FOR THE PIE DOUGH
⅞ CUP (100G) ALL-PURPOSE FLOUR,
PLUS EXTRA FOR DUSTING

2 TABLESPOONS SUPERFINE SUGAR

5½ TABLESPOONS (80G),
CUBED, PLUS EXTRA FOR GREASING

1 TABLESPOON BEATEN EGG

FOR THE SACHER SPONGE CAKE
5OZ (140G) CHOCOLATE (70% cocoa solids),
BROKEN INTO PIECES

⅔ CUP (150G) UNSALTED BUTTER, CUBED,
ROOM TEMPERATURE

½ CUP (50G) CONFECTIONERS' SUGAR, SIFTED

6 MEDIUM EGGS, SEPARATED

½ CUP SUPERFINE SUGAR

1 CUP (120G) ALL-PURPOSE FLOUR

¼ CUP (20G) COCOA POWDER

FOR THE GLAZE AND FILLING
14OZ (400G) ORANGE MARMALADE

3½ TABLESPOONS UNSALTED BUTTER

7OZ (200G) DARK CHOCOLATE
(70% cocoa solids)

¾ CUP (180ML) WATER

1½ CUPS (300G) SUPERFINE SUGAR

CHOCOLATE FOR PIPING, AS NEEDED

In the cake display of a German café, the Sacher Torte always stuck out for me. With its thick chocolate coating, dense sponge cakes, and minimalist filling, it had a promise of something different, and on occasion I would forgo my usual favorites and have a Sacher with a dollop of whipped cream. In its classic form, the rich, dark chocolate flavor is perfectly balanced with sweet apricot jam.

Since coming to England, I have really learned to appreciate orange marmalade, and for many years now I have been making my own Seville orange marmalade. Switching apricot for Seville orange introduces a light bitterness, creating a surprisingly different cake.

For the pie dough, put all the ingredients in a bowl and mix with your hands until the dough is smooth. Wrap in plastic wrap and set aside in the fridge for about 30 minutes, until the dough is just firm enough to roll out.

Preheat the oven to 375°F (190°C). Lightly grease a 10in (25cm) cake pan or sandwich pan.

On a floured surface, roll out the dough to a circle about ⅛in (3mm) thick. Transfer the dough to the pan, cutting off any surplus, since only the bottom needs to be covered. Prick the pie crust with a fork so that trapped air can escape during baking. Bake for 8–10 minutes, until the edges start to brown.

For the Sacher sponge cake, melt the chocolate. Don't let it get too hot. You can set a plastic or metal bowl with the chocolate over a saucepan of water that has just boiled.

Line the bottom of a 10in (25cm) springform cake pan with parchment paper and grease the sides. Reduce the oven temperature 350°F (180°C).

Put the butter and confectioners' sugar in a bowl and beat until frothy. Beat in the egg yolks one by one. Slowly whisk in the melted chocolate.

Beat the egg whites to soft peaks, then gradually beat in the sugar and continue to beat until stiff peaks form and the egg whites are shiny. Sift the flour and cocoa powder toge ther. Fold one-third of the egg whites into the butter mixture. Then fold in the flour and cocoa powder. Finally, fold in the remaining egg whites.

Transfer the batter to the prepared pan, spread evenly and bake for 45 minutes, until a skewer inserted in the center comes out clean. Leave the sponge cake to cool in the pan for 30 minutes, then remove from the pan, peel off the parchment paper, and let cool completely.

Once cool, cut the sponge cake in half horizontally and trim the top, if necessary, to get an even sponge cake.

To assemble, lightly heat the marmalade so that it gets a bit runny. Add a bit of water, if necessary. Place the pie crust on a cake board and thinly cover it with marmalade. Place the bottom sponge cake on top of the pie crust and cover the sponge cake thinly with marmalade. (I've found that having a bit of peel in this layer adds a nice texture.) Put the remaining sponge cake on top. Strain the marmalade and cover the whole cake thinly with it.

To make the glaze, which is a classic chocolate icing called *konserve-schokolade*, put the butter and chocolate into a bowl—I like to use thin plastic or metal bowls because they transfer the heat quickly. Place the bowl over a saucepan with water that has just boiled. The bowl shouldn't touch the water.

Put the water and sugar into a saucepan and bring to a boil while stirring. Continue boiling the syrup, without stirring, until it reaches 226°F (108°C). Take the syrup off the heat and slowly add the chocolate mixture while stirring. Put the glaze back on the heat and boil, stirring constantly, until the glaze reaches 219°F (104°C).

Take off the heat and gently stir while the glaze is cooling and thickening. The consistency should be such that some glaze poured over the back of a metal spoon sets about ⅛in (4mm) thick; the temperature of the glaze will be about 113°F (45°C).

Pour the glaze over the cake and spread it with a pastry knife so that the top and the sides of the cake are evenly covered. Leave the glaze to set.

To decorate, pipe chocolate ornaments, or the words "Almost Sacher" on top.

This cake keeps extremely well and does not need cooling. Hotel Sacher sends its cakes worldwide, as they can keep for weeks in an airtight container.

Prinzregenten-Torte

This cake was created in honor of the Bavarian Prince Regent Luitpold in the nineteenth century. The layers symbolize the eight counties of Bavaria at the time. The build of this cake is very similar to the Herren-Torte on page 51, which was invented much later. This cake contains no alcohol, and the strongly contrasting layers make it a feast for the eyes as well as for the palate.

serves 12

FOR THE SPONGE CAKES
6 MEDIUM EGGS, SEPARATED

⅞ CUP (175G) SUPERFINE SUGAR

¾ CUP (90G) ALL-PURPOSE FLOUR

¾ CUP (85G) CORNSTARCH

¼ CUP (60G) UNSALTED BUTTER, MELTED

FOR THE CHOCOLATE BUTTERCREAM
4OZ (120G) DARK CHOCOLATE
(70% cocoa solids), BROKEN INTO PIECES

1 CUP + 2 TABLESPOONS UNSALTED BUTTER,
ROOM TEMPERATURE

2 MEDIUM EGG YOLKS

1¼ CUPS (150G) CONFECTIONERS' SUGAR

FOR THE GLAZE
7OZ (200G) CHOCOLATE (54% cocoa solids),
BROKEN INTO PIECES

3½ TABLESPOONS UNSALTED BUTTER

For the sponge cakes, prepare eight sheets of parchment paper. Using a pencil, draw a circle of 10in (25cm) diameter on each of the sheets of paper. Turn the paper upside down so that the batter won't come into contact with the pencil.

Preheat the oven to 425°F (22°C).

Divide the eggs whites and yolks between two big heatproof bowls. Pour half the sugar into the yolks. Beat the egg whites to soft peaks. Slowly add the remaining sugar bit by bit and whip to stiff peaks.

Sift the flour and cornstarch together.

Over a pan of boiling water, beat the sugar and egg yolks until they have a temperature of about 110°F (43°C). Remove the bowl and continue beating until the egg yolks are pale, frothy, and creamy. Fold one-third of the egg white into the egg yolks. Then fold in the remaining egg white. Fold in the flour mixture, followed by the melted butter.

The batter is enough for eight sponge cakes. Depending on your equipment, you can bake up to three in one batch.

Spread the batter thinly inside the circles on the parchment paper. Transfer the parchment paper onto baking pans and bake for 6–8 minutes. Don't overbake; the thin sponge cakes can dry out very quickly and get brittle.

Leave to cool and repeat the previous steps until you have baked all eight sponge cakes.

For the chocolate buttercream, melt the chocolate in a heatproof bowl over boiling water, making sure the bowl does not touch the water below (this is called a double boiler). Once the chocolate has melted, set aside.

Beat the butter until light and pale, then add egg yolks and confectioners' sugar bit by bit while beating. Continue beating until the mixture is very light and frothy. Continue beating while very slowly adding the liquid chocolate. Set aside.

To assemble the cake, make sure all eight sponge cakes are the same size. Trim them, if necessary.

Place the bottom sponge cake on a cake plate and thinly cover with chocolate buttercream. Place the next one on top of the buttercream and coat thinly. Continue in this way until you have used all the sponge cakes. Use buttercream to cover the sides and the top of the cake; only a very thin layer is necessary to even out little irregularities. Put the cake in the fridge for at least 30 minutes.

Once the cake is cool and the buttercream is set, prepare the glaze. Melt the chocolate and butter over a double boiler. Once melted, take the glaze off the heat and carefully stir the glaze while it is cooling. When it has the right consistency to cover the back of a spoon, apply the chocolate glaze to the cake, either using a brush, or by pouring. Leave the glaze to set.

Mark the cake slices lightly with the back of a knife. For decoration, pipe a pirouette of chocolate buttercream onto each slice. This cake improves in flavor over time and keeps very well in an airtight container for at least 3 days.

Mango-Maracuja Sahnetorte
Passion Fruit and Mango Charlotte Royale

I have always been attracted to the Charlotte royales they had in those big department-store cake displays. Curiously, I have never had one! But I've ̶ *this opportunity to share my recipe for this stunning cake with its 1970s fr* ̶ *The Genoese sponge cake forms the base of this cake, while the Joconde spo* ̶ *cake creates the swirled pattern.*

serves 16

FOR THE GENOESE SPONGE CAKE
4 MEDIUM EGGS

⅔ CUP (125G) SUPERFINE SUGAR

1 CUP + 1 TABLESPOON (125G)
ALL-PURPOSE FLOUR

2 TABLESPOONS UNSALTED BUTTER, MELTED

FOR THE JOCONDE SPONGE CAKE
3½OZ (100G) GROUND ALMONDS

⅔ CUP (65G) CONFECTIONERS' SUGAR, SIFTED

⅓ CUP (35G) ALL-PURPOSE FLOUR

3 LARGE EGGS

1 LARGE EGG YOLK

3 LARGE EGG WHITES

2½ TABLESPOONS SUPERFINE SUGAR

2½ TABLESPOONS UNSALTED BUTTER, MELTED

To make the Genoese sponge cake, line a 15 x 10in (38 x 25cm) baking pan with parchment paper.

Preheat the oven to 375°F (190°C).

Put the eggs and sugar in a heatproof bowl. Place over a pan of boiling water and beat until the egg mix has reached 85°F (30°C) or has doubled in volume. Take the egg mixture off the heat and beat until the eggs are at room temperature—this takes about 10 minutes.

Fold in the flour, then fold in the melted butter. Transfer the batter to the prepared pan and carefully even out the batter. Bake for about 8–10 minutes. The sponge cake should begin to turn golden and spring back when gently touched. For cooling, remove the sponge cake with the parchment paper from the pan and place it on a wire rack.

To make the Joconde sponge cake, line a baking pan with parchment paper. Increase the oven temperature to 425°F (220°C).

In a large bowl, mix together the ground almonds, confectioners' sugar and flour. Add the whole eggs and incorporate them. Add the egg yolk.

In a separate bowl, beat the egg whites to soft peaks. Add the sugar and continue beating the egg whites to stiff peaks. Fold one-third of the egg whites into the flour and egg mixture, then fold in the remaining egg whites. Finally, fold in the melted butter.

continued

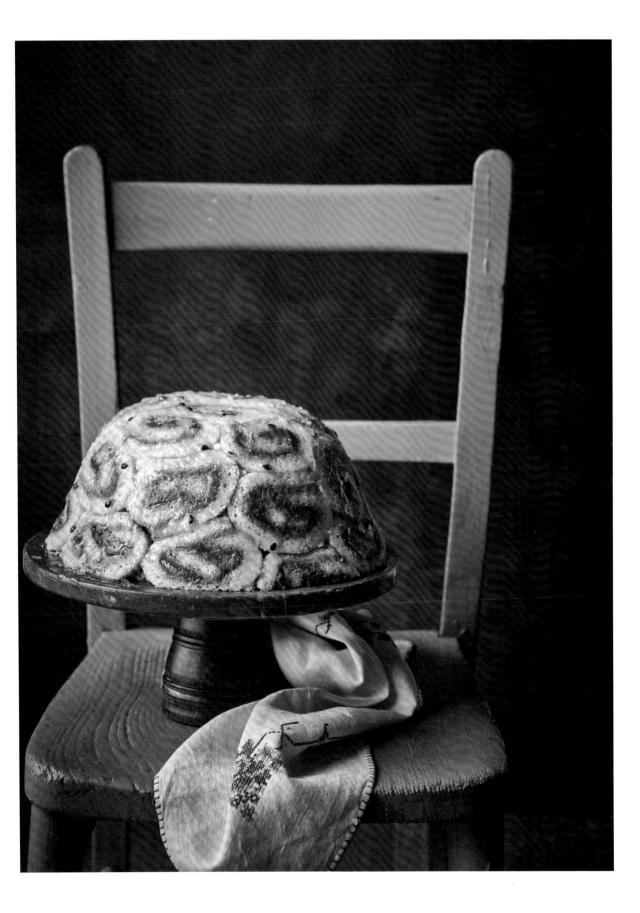

FOR THE CARAMEL FILLING
1¼ CUPS (250G) SUPERFINE SUGAR

⅓ CUP (80ML) WATER

5OZ (150ML) HEAVY CREAM

5½ TABLESPOONS UNSALTED BUTTER

FOR THE PASSION FRUIT
AND MANGO BAVARIAN CREAM
3 X ¼OZ (7G) ENVELOPES GELATIN POWDER

4 TABLESPOONS WATER

9 PASSION FRUIT

1 MANGO, RIPE

⅞ CUP (160G) SUPERFINE SUGAR

2½ CUPS (600ML) HEAVY CREAM

FOR THE PASSION FRUIT GLAZE
2 X ¼OZ (7G) ENVELOPES GELATIN POWDER

1 PASSION FRUIT

3½OZ (100ML) WATER

3 TABLESPOONS SUPERFINE SUGAR

Spread the batter on the parchment paper into a rectangle of about 14 x 10in (35 x 25cm). Bake for about 8 minutes. Transfer the sponge cake with the parchment paper onto a wire rack and cover with a second sheet of parchment paper to prevent the cake from drying out. Set aside and leave to cool.

To make the caramel, put the sugar and water into a pan and bring gently to a boil while stirring. Boil the sugar without stirring until it turns a rich golden-brown. Take off the heat, immediately add heavy cream and butter, and stir. Be very careful; the hot caramel will bubble up and might splash. Pour into a heatproof bowl and set aside to cool.

To assemble the shell, line a 2–3 quart (2–3 liter) bowl with plastic wrap. Take your cool Joconde sponge cake, still on the parchment paper, and place it on your work surface with a long edge toward you. Spread the caramel thinly on the Joconde, leaving a small strip uncovered along the far side. Roll the Joconde tightly, starting with the edge closest to you. Use the parchment paper as an aid to roll tightly, and while rolling, remove it from the sponge cake bit by bit.

Cut the roll into slices about ¼in (6mm) thick. Line the inside of the bowl with a layer of the slices. Push them in place so that no gaps remain, if possible. The edge will be trimmed—it can be uneven at this point. Set aside.

To make the passion fruit and mango Bavarian cream, sprinkle the gelatin over the water and set aside.

Pass the pulp of the passion fruit through a sieve. Reserve some of the seeds for the filling.

Peel the mango, cut off the flesh around the pit. Blend the mango fruit flesh until very smooth. Add the juice from the passion fruit, and some seeds if required. You will need 15oz (420g) of fruit pulp. If you have less, add some water or fruit juice.

Transfer the fruit pulp to a pan, add the sugar, and bring to a boil. Take the pulp off the heat, add the gelatin, and stir until the gelatin is completely dissolved, then let cool.

Once the pulp has cooled and the gelatin is starting to set, beat the heavy cream. It should be stiff, but smooth. Don't overbeat or it is hard to fold it into the fruit pulp.

Fold the heavy cream into the fruit pulp, first one-third of the cream and then the rest. Pour the Bavarian cream into the cake-lined bowl and level with a palette knife or spatula.

Cut a lid out of the Genoese sponge cake that fits well on top of the Bavarian cream and place it on top of the cream, slightly pressing down and leveling the cake. This will become the bottom. Put the cake into the fridge for at least 2 hours.

To make the glaze, sprinkle the gelatin over the water and set aside. Put the passion fruit pulp with seeds into a food processor and give it a short burst, but be careful not to destroy the seeds. Put the pulp into a small saucepan and add the remaining ingredients for the glaze, except for the gelatin. Bring the pulp mixture to a boil, then remove from the heat and stir in the gelatin until completely dissolved. Leave to cool.

Remove the cake from the fridge. Trim any excess cake around the edge.

To remove the Charlotte from the bowl, turn it upside down onto a cake plate or cake stand. Remove the plastic wrap.

Once the glaze starts setting, pour it over the Charlotte to cover it evenly.

Keep the cake in the fridge until you are ready to serve. Store in the fridge and consume within 2 days.

Triple Charlotte Russe

serves 16

FOR THE GENOESE SPONGE CAKE
4 MEDIUM EGGS

¾ CUP (125G) SUPERFINE SUGAR

1 CUP +1 TABLESPOON (125G)
ALL-PURPOSE FLOUR

1¾ TABLESPOONS UNSALTED BUTTER, MELTED

FOR THE LADYFINGERS
3 MEDIUM EGGS, SEPARATED

½ CUP (90G) SUPERFINE SUGAR

¾ CUP (90G) ALL-PURPOSE FLOUR

1 TABLESPOON ORANGE BLOSSOM WATER

CONFECTIONERS' SUGAR FOR DUSTING

FOR THE BLUEBERRY BAVARIAN CREAM
9OZ (250G) BLUEBERRIES, FROZEN OR FRESH

¼ CUP (60ML) WATER

2 X ¼OZ (7G) ENVELOPES GELATIN POWDER

3 TABLESPOONS SUPERFINE SUGAR

7OZ (200ML) HEAVY CREAM

FOR THE RASPBERRY BAVARIAN CREAM
¾LB (350G) RASPBERRIES, FROZEN OR FRESH

¼ CUP (60ML) WATER WATER

2 X ¼OZ (7G) ENVELOPES GELATIN POWDER

3 TABLESPOONS SUPERFINE SUGAR

7OZ (200ML) HEAVY CREAM

This is a multilayered, rich, and colorful cake for special occasions. It takes some effort to make, but, since the sponge cake and ladyfingers can be made a day in advance, effort can be spread out. It is important with this cake, as with all Charlotte-style cakes, to have enough time and space for proper cooling.

To make the Genoese sponge cake base, line a 15 x 10in (38 x 25cm) baking pan with parchment paper. Preheat the oven to 375°F (190°C).

Put the eggs and sugar in a heatproof bowl. Place over a pan of boiling water and beat until the egg mix has reached 85°F (30°C) or has doubled in volume. Take the egg mixture off the heat and beat until the eggs are at room temperature—this takes about 10 minutes.

Fold in the flour, then fold in the melted butter. Transfer the batter to the prepared pan and carefully even out the batter. Bake for about 8–10 minutes. The sponge cake should begin to turn golden and spring back when gently touched. Remove the sponge cake with the parchment paper from the pan and let cool on a wire rack.

To make the ladyfingers, line two baking pans with parchment paper or silicone sheets. Increase the oven to 425°F (220°C).

Beat the egg whites to soft peaks. Add one-third of the sugar and continue beating until the meringue is smooth and shiny.

In a large bowl, beat the egg yolks with the remaining sugar until they turn frothy, creamy, and pale. Add one-third of the meringue to the egg yolks and fold it in. Sift the flour over the egg mixture and fold it in. Add the orange blossom water and the remaining meringue and fold in.

Transfer the batter to a piping bag with a medium plain nozzle. Pipe straight lines of 3in (7cm) length onto the baking sheets. Lightly dust the ladyfingers with confectioners' sugar.

Bake the ladyfingers for about 8 minutes, until they start turning golden. Leave to cool on a wire rack.

continued

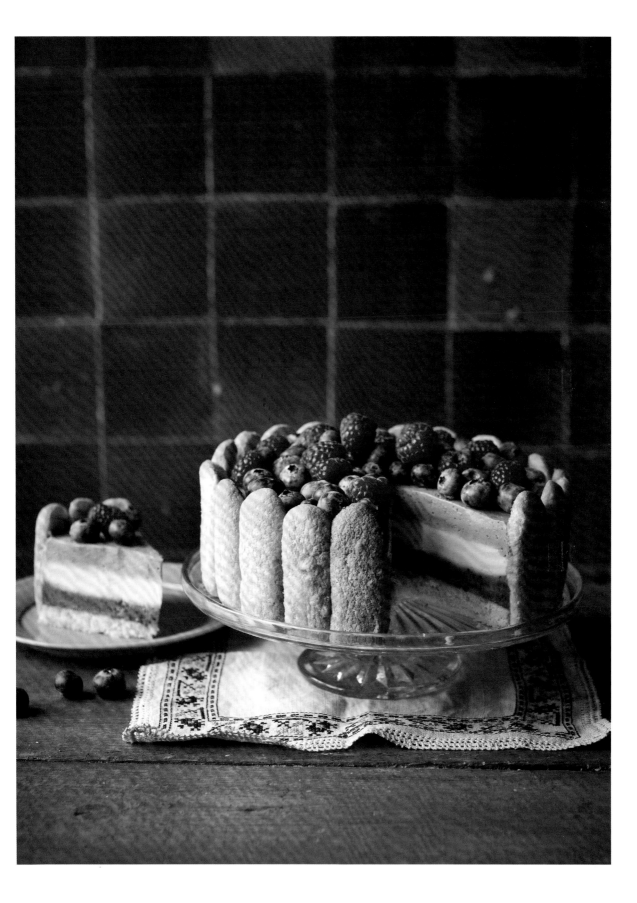

FOR THE WHITE CHOCOLATE
BAVARIAN CREAM
2 X ¼OZ (7G) ENVELOPES GELATIN POWDER

¼ CUP (60ML) WATER

1 MEDIUM EGG YOLK

½ TEASPOON CORNSTARCH

8OZ (225G) WHITE CHOCOLATE

½ CUP (130ML) WHOLE MILK

7OZ (200ML) HEAVY CREAM

FOR DECORATION
FRESH FRUIT, AS REQUIRED

HEAVY CREAM, AS REQUIRED

CONFECTIONERS' SUGAR, AS REQUIRED

FOR THE GLAZE (optional)
2 X ¼OZ (7G) ENVELOPES GELATIN POWDER

3½OZ (100ML) WATER

1OZ (20ML) RASPBERRY LIQUEUR
OR SIMILAR

3 TABLESPOONS SUPERFINE SUGAR

For the three layers of Bavarian cream, timing is essential. Before adding a new layer of Bavarian cream, the previous layer needs to be set. This is best accomplished by letting the Bavarian cream almost set before adding it to the cake. This also prevents spills through little gaps between the ladyfingers.

To prepare the fruit pulps for the fruit Bavarian creams, put the blueberries and raspberries into separate pans, add 1 tablespoon of water to each, and bring the berries to a boil. Simmer for about 5 minutes, then leave to cool. Pass the berries through a sieve and measure the amount of raspberry pulp and blueberry pulp. You need 4½oz (130g) of each pulp.

To assemble the sponge cakes, cut a 9½in (24cm) diameter circle out of your sponge cake sheet ½in (1cm) less than a 10in (25cm) springform pan. Place the sponge disk on the bottom of the pan.

Cut one end of the ladyfingers so that they sit around the sides of the pan, with the intact ends level with the top. Place the ladyfingers around the edge, leaving no gaps.

To prepare the blueberry Bavarian cream, sprinkle the gelatin over the water and set aside.

Heat the blueberry pulp with the sugar until it starts boiling. Take off the heat, stir in the gelatin and let it cool. Once the pulp has cooled and the gelatin is starting to set, whip the heavy cream. It should be stiff, but smooth. Don't overbeat, or it is hard to fold it into the fruit pulp.

Fold the heavy cream into the fruit pulp, first adding one-third and then the remaining cream. Pour the blueberry Bavarian cream onto the cake base, sprinkle with some fresh blueberries, if desired, and level using a small palette knife. Put the cake into the fridge or freezer.

To prepare the white chocolate Bavarian cream, sprinkle the gelatin over the water and set aside. In a small bowl, mix the egg yolk with the cornstarch. Set aside. Break the white chocolate into a heatproof bowl and set aside.

Heat the milk to scalding point. Take it off the heat and pour one-third of the hot milk into the egg yolk while stirring. Pour the egg yolk and milk back to the remaining milk in the pan, stirring constantly. Gently heat until it starts to thicken.

Add the gelatin and stir until the gelatin is dissolved. Pour the hot milk mixture over the white chocolate and let it sit for a couple of minutes. Next, stir the chocolate until it is completely dissolved and the mixture is homogeneous. Set aside to cool.

Once the chocolate mixture is cool and starts to thicken, beat the heavy cream. It should be stiff, but smooth. Don't overbeat or it is hard to fold it into the chocolate mixture.

Fold the heavy cream into the chocolate mixture, first adding one-third and then the remaining cream. Take the cake out of the fridge/freezer. Pour the white chocolate Bavarian cream onto the blueberry layer and level using a small palette knife. Put the cake back into the fridge or freezer.

To prepare the raspberry Bavarian cream, sprinkle the gelatin over the water and set aside.

Heat the raspberry pulp with the sugar until it starts boiling. Take off the heat, stir in the gelatin, and let it cool. Once the pulp has cooled and the gelatin is starting to set, beat the heavy cream. It should be stiff, but smooth. Don't overbeat or it is hard to fold it into the fruit pulp.

Fold the heavy cream into the fruit pulp, first adding one-third and then the remaining cream. Take the cake out of the fridge/freezer. Pour the raspberry Bavarian cream onto the white chocolate layer, sprinkle with fresh raspberries, if desired, level using a small palette knife. Put the cake back into the fridge or freezer.

Once the raspberry cream has set sufficiently, decorate the cake by arranging fresh fruit on top of the raspberry layer. If the cake is to be kept, prepare a glaze. Sprinkle the gelatin over the water and set aside. Heat the raspberry liqueur and sugar to about 185°F (85°F). Take off the heat and add the gelatin. Stir until the gelatin is dissolved.

Let the glaze cool until it starts to set, then pour it carefully over the fruit. If the cake is to be eaten on the same day, you can omit the glaze and add decorations using piped whipped cream. You can also sprinkle the fruit with confectioners' sugar. Keep the cake in the fridge for at least 1 hour before serving to make sure all the layers are set. Remove from the pan just before serving. This cake must be kept in the fridge. Consume within 2 to 3 days.

serves 12

FOR THE PIE DOUGH

2½ CUPS (300G) ALL-PURPOSE FLOUR

⅓ CUP (35G) GROUND ALMONDS

½ CUP + 1 TABLESPOON (110G) SUPERFINE SUGAR

1 PINCH SALT

¾ CUP (180G) UNSALTED BUTTER, COLD, CUBED,
PLUS EXTRA FOR GREASING

2 TEASPOONS VANILLA BEAN PASTE

1 MEDIUM EGG

FOR THE FILLING

1¾OZ (50G) RAISINS (ABOUT ⅓ CUP) RAISINS

RUM, AS NEEDED TO COVER RAISINS

4 MEDIUM EGGS, SEPARATED

1 PINCH SALT

3½OZ (100ML) HEAVY CREAM

26OZ (750G) LOW-FAT QUARK

5½OZ (150G) SOUR CREAM

⅞ CUP (180G) SUPERFINE SUGAR

⅓ CUP (40G) CORNSTARCH

1 TEASPOON VANILLA BEAN PASTE

ZEST OF 1 LEMON

Käsekuchen
Cheesecake with Raisins

When I developed this recipe, my wife said, "Why have you never made such a delicious thing before?!" My answer was that I didn't have the right recipe. I developed this to combine the richness of a 1950s cheesecake with a twenty-first-century method. This type of cheesecake is one of my all-time favorite cakes. The filling is smooth and creamy, and the raisins add a bit of texture. As with most German baked cheesecakes, this one uses quark as main ingredient for the filling.

Put the raisins in a bowl and add just enough rum to cover them. Cover the bowl and set aside to soak, ideally overnight. To speed up the soaking, you can heat the rum and raisins gently in a microwave—don't boil them.

For the pie dough, put the flour, almonds, sugar, and salt in a bowl and mix together. Add the butter, vanilla bean paste, and egg. Knead until a smooth ball of dough forms. Wrap in plastic wrap and let it rest in the fridge for at least 30 minutes.

Preheat the oven to 350°F (180°C).

Once the dough has rested, line the bottom of a 10in (25cm) springform cake pan with parchment paper. Grease the sides of the pan with butter.

Roll the pastry into a disk to line the pan. There should be a rim of about 2in (5cm) all around the sides. Prepare the pie crust for blind baking, using your usual method (ceramic beans or dried beans). Blind bake the pie crust for 25 minutes. Remove from the oven and leave to cool.

While the pie crust is baking, prepare the filling. Put the egg whites in a bowl, add the salt, and beat to soft peaks. Don't overbeat, or it will be harder to fold the egg whites into the mixture. Set aside.

Put the heavy cream into a bowl and beat until stiff. Set aside.

Put the remaining ingredients for the filling, except the rum and raisins, into a big bowl and mix, using a hand mixer or a stand mixer fitted with balloon whisk, until smooth. Fold in one-third of the egg whites to break up the quark mix—this makes it a lot easier to fold in the remaining egg whites. Fold in the remaining egg whites. Finally, fold in the whipped cream.

Drain the raisins.

By now the pie crust should be done and should have cooled a bit. Spread one-third of the filling evenly over the crust bottom. Sprinkle about half of the raisins over the filling. Add another one-third of the filling, sprinkle over the remaining raisins, then add the remaining filling.

Bake for about 1 hour in the lower third of the oven. Take care that the filling doesn't burn. If it gets dark with some time to go, cover the cake with foil.

Once done, let the cake cool before removing from the pan. This cake keeps well in the fridge for several days. It is great eaten right away, but will even be better the next day.

Versunkener Apfelkuchen
Sunken Apple Cake

This apple cake is one of the easiest to make, and one of the most satisfying German cakes. It was a staple at our Sunday Kaffee & Kuchen *(Coffee & Cake) events. There wasn't a village fete with a bake sale where there weren't several versions of this cake on offer. The appearance with the cut apple pieces is very typical. But this cake also lends itself to other fruit—it works well with rhubarb, fresh cherries, gooseberries, or red currants.*

Preheat the oven to 350°F (180°C).

Peel, quarter, and core the apples. Make about 10 incisions lengthwise in the "outside" of each apple piece. Put the apples in a bowl, together with the cinnamon and teaspoon of sugar, stir to cover the apples, and set aside.

Grease a 9in (23cm) springform cake pan and line the bottom with parchment paper.

Put the sugar and butter into a bowl and beat until light and frothy. Add the eggs one at a time and beat to incorporate. Add the lemon zest. Stir in the milk. Sift the flour, baking powder, and cardamom together and incorporate into the butter and eggs bit by bit. Spread the batter evenly in the prepared pan.

Lay the apple quarters on top (with the "insides" down, so that the cuts are visible) and slightly press them down into the batter. Bake for about 45 minutes, until a skewer inserted into the center comes out clean. Leave to cool for about 10 minutes, then remove from the pan.

Glaze the cake with apricot jam, or once cool, dust the cake with confectioners' sugar.

This cake keeps very well for 4 days in an airtight container and improves in flavor after a day.

serves 12

5 APPLES
(tart and firm, such as Granny Smith)

1 TEASPOON GROUND CINNAMON

⅔ CUP (120G) SUPERFINE SUGAR,
PLUS 1 TEASPOON FOR THE APPLES

9 TABLESPOONS (125G) UNSALTED BUTTER,
OR MARGARINE, ROOM TEMPERATURE,
PLUS EXTRA FOR GREASING

3 MEDIUM EGGS, ROOM TEMPERATURE

ZEST OF 1 LEMON

1¾ CUPS (200G) ALL-PURPOSE FLOUR

3½ TEASPOONS BAKING POWDER

½ TEASPOON GROUND CARDAMOM

1 TABLESPOON WHOLE MILK

APRICOT JAM OR CONFECTIONERS' SUGAR
FOR FINISHING

serves 12

FOR THE SPONGE CAKE
¼ CUP (60G) UNSALTED BUTTER,
PLUS EXTRA FOR GREASING

¾ CUP (80G) ALL-PURPOSE FLOUR

80G CORNSTARCH

3 TEASPOONS BAKING POWDER

4 MEDIUM EGGS

⅔ CUP (125G) SUPERFINE SUGAR

CONFECTIONERS' SUGAR FOR DUSTING

FOR THE FILLING
3½OZ (100ML) WATER

2 X ¼OZ (7G) ENVELOPES GELATIN POWDER

⅔ CUP (150ML) WHOLE MILK

¾ CUP (150G) SUPERFINE SUGAR

4 MEDIUM EGG YOLKS

1 LEMON
26OZ (750G) LOW-FAT QUARK

17OZ (500ML) HEAVY CREAM

Käsesahne-Torte

*Despite the very similar name, this cake is very different from the Käsekuchen on
page 67. Sandwiched between two thin layers of sponge cake is a thick layer of a cold
set filling, which you could describe as a kind of Bavarian cream containing quark.
The combination of quark and lemon is found in many German pastries and cakes.
Often, canned mandarin slices are added to the quark filling to give the cake some
color, and in that case the top can be decorated with mandarin slices as well.*

*This cake is very light and has a refreshing mouthfeel. For me, it was always
tough to decide between baked cheesecake and Käsesahne-Torte (once Black Forest
gateau had been ruled out).*

The sponge cake can be prepared the day before
assembling the cake. Grease and line a 10in (25cm)
springform cake pan with parchment paper. Preheat
the oven to 400°F (200°C).

Melt the butter in a microwave or over hot water.
Sift the flour, cornstarch, and baking powder
together and set aside.

Put the eggs and sugar into a bowl and beat with
a hand mixer or using a stand mixer fitted with
the balloon whisk attachment, until the yolks have
become thick and creamy (ribbon stage).

Fold in the flour mixture, then the melted butter.
Transfer the batter to the prepared pan, spread
it evenly, and bake for about 35 minutes, until a
skewer inserted into the center comes out clean. Let
the sponge cake cool in the pan for 10 minutes, then
remove it from the pan and let it cool completely.

Once you are ready to assemble the cake, make sure
you have enough space in your fridge for the cake.
Cut the sponge cake in half horizontally so that you
get two even layers of equal thickness.

Put the bottom layer of sponge cake into a 10in
(25cm) springform cake pan. Now line the sides of
the pan with parchment paper or plastic wrap. Set
aside. Put the water into a wide bowl and sprinkle
the gelatin over it.

Put the milk, sugar, egg yolks, zest from the lemon,
and 2 teaspoons of lemon juice into a saucepan and
heat until it thickens very lightly. It should have
reached a temperature of 185°F (85°C) at this point.
Take the saucepan off the heat, add the gelatin and
water mixture and stir gently until all the gelatin is
dissolved. Let cool until lukewarm and the gelatin
starts to set.

Meanwhile, put the quark into a bowl and beat until
smooth. Pour the heavy cream into a large bowl.

When the egg-gelatin mixture is ready, beat the
cream to soft peaks. Don't overbeat or it will be
harder to fold it into the egg mixture. Fold the
quark and whipped cream into the egg mixture bit
by bit. Add in a bit more lemon juice, if desired.

Transfer the filling onto the bottom layer of sponge
cake and spread it evenly. Work quickly because the
filling might set. Place the top sponge cake layer onto
the filling and press it gently. Put the pan into the
fridge for at least 3 hours, or overnight, if possible.

Just before the cake is needed, take it out of the
pan, sprinkle the with confectioners' sugar, and
mark 16 pieces with either a cake divider or the
back of a knife.

This cake keeps for several days stored in the fridge.

Russischer Zupfkuchen
Russian Plucked Cake

The literal translation for this recipe is "Russian pulled cake." It is a baked cheesecake with a chocolate crust, and some of the chocolate pastry is pulled apart and sprinkled over the top. This gives the slices a very attractive black-and-white look, and there is a beautiful contrast in both texture and flavor, which you experience with every bite.

serves 12

FOR THE DOUGH
2⅓ CUPS (280G) ALL-PURPOSE FLOUR

½ CUP (40G) COCOA POWDER

2 TEASPOONS BAKING POWDER

⅔ CUP (125G) SUPERFINE SUGAR

1 MEDIUM EGG

⅔ CUP (150G) UNSALTED BUTTER,
ROOM TEMPERATURE,
PLUS EXTRA FOR GREASING

ZEST OF 1 MEDIUM ORANGE

FOR THE FILLING
1 CUP + 2 TABLESPOONS (250G)
UNSALTED BUTTER, MELTED

18OZ (500G) LOW-FAT QUARK,
ROOM TEMPERATURE

¾ CUP (150G) SUPERFINE SUGAR

2 TEASPOONS VANILLA BEAN PASTE

3 MEDIUM EGGS

⅓ CUP (40G) CORNSTARCH

For the dough, sift the flour, cocoa powder, and baking powder together in a bowl. Add the remaining dough ingredients and mix with your hands until the dough forms a smooth ball. Wrap the dough in plastic wrap and chill in the fridge for at least 30 minutes. While the dough is resting, prepare the filling and the pan. Grease a 10in (25cm) springform cake pan with butter, or line it with parchment paper.

Preheat the oven to 350°F (180°C).

Melt the butter in a microwave or in a saucepan on the stovetop. Make sure it doesn't get too hot—it should be lukewarm when being used.

While the butter is cooling, take two-thirds of the chocolate dough and roll it out slightly bigger than the diameter of the cake pan. It should be big enough to get a 1in (2cm) rim around the sides. Line the pan with the chocolate dough.

Combine all the filling ingredients in a bowl and beat until smooth. Spread the filling evenly in the lined pan, ideally not covering the rim.

Take the remaining chocolate dough, pull it into rough pieces and sprinkle them over the filling. Don't attempt to cover the whole area; you get the best effect if plenty of white filling shines through the gaps. Bake for about 1 hour in the bottom third of the oven.

Leave the cake to cool in the pan for 10 minutes, then transfer it to a wire rack to cool completely. This cake keeps very well, and it improves for the first 2 days after baking. Keep in an airtight container for up to 3 days.

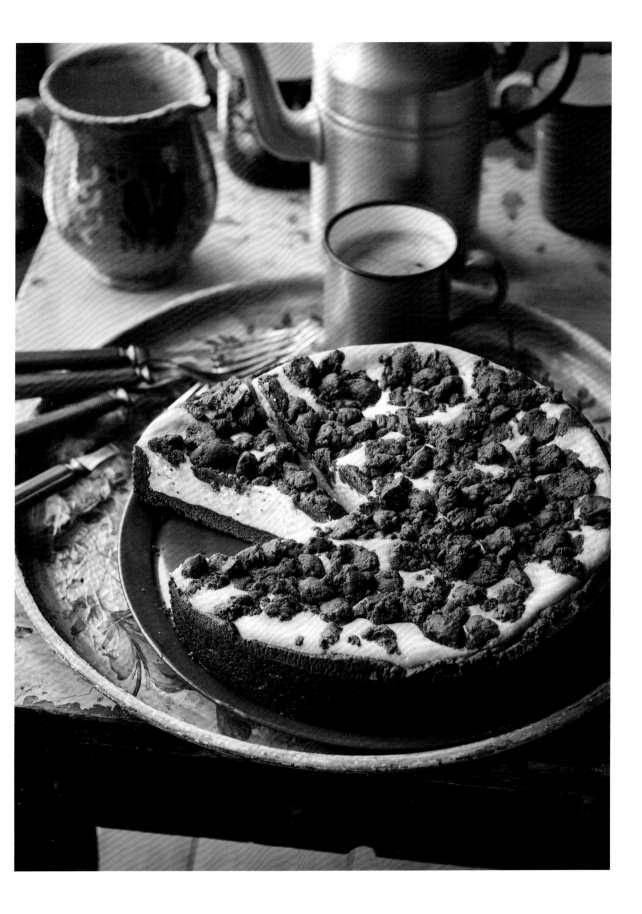

Zwetschgen-Kuchen
Plum Tart with Streusel

serves 12

FOR THE CRUST
2 CUPS (250G) ALL-PURPOSE FLOUR,
PLUS EXTRA FOR DUSTING

9 TABLESPOONS (125G) UNSALTED BUTTER,
CUBED, PLUS EXTRA FOR GREASING

⅓ CUP SUPERFINE SUGAR

2 TEASPOONS
STRONG VANILLA SUGAR (PAGE 180)

ZEST OF 1 LEMON

1 MEDIUM EGG

1 PINCH SALT

1 EGG YOLK FOR GLAZING

FOR THE TOPPING
ABOUT 2LB (1KG) PLUMS

⅔ CUPS (75G) ALL-PURPOSE FLOUR

½ CUP (50G) GROUND ALMONDS

½ CUP (100G) GRANULATED SUGAR

6½ TABLESPOONS (100G)
UNSALTED BUTTER, CUBED

½ TEASPOON GROUND CINNAMON

This cake used to be seasonal, and always highly anticipated. In our huge garden we had three plum trees, and in some years, they carried so much fruit that the branches had to be supported. Everybody looked forward to the harvest, and after eating the ripe fruit directly from the trees, plum tarts in all their variations were a highlight of the season.

This recipe is quite simple, but very tasty. Depending on the type of plums, the tart can get a bit juicy. The amount of streusel seems small, since this cake shouldn't be completely covered.

Preheat the oven to 375°F (190°C). Grease and line a 10in (25cm) springform cake pan with parchment paper.

Put all the ingredients for the crust, except the egg yolk, into a bowl. With your hands, mix and work the ingredients together until the dough becomes smooth and pliable. On a floured surface, roll out the dough slightly larger than the diameter of the pan. Transfer the dough to the pan—there should be a rim of about 1in (3cm) around the sides. Brush the inside of the crust with egg yolk.

Prepare the plums. Wash them, halve them, and remove the pits. Then, from the cut side, cut them again about halfway through. Arrange the plums on the crust.

For the streusel, add the remaining topping ingredients to a bowl and mix and work the dough with your hands until the dough holds together in big chunks. Spread the chunks randomly over the plums, leaving part of the plums uncovered.

Bake for about 1 hour, 10 minutes. Keep an eye on the color of the streusel and don't let it get too dark.

This cake tastes great warm, and whipped cream or vanilla ice cream are good accompaniments. It keeps well for several days stored in an airtight container.

Johannisbeer-Kuchen mit Baiser
Red Currant Tart with Meringue

My parents always grew red currants in their garden and, like so many other fruit cakes, this was—and still is—a seasonal favorite.

Preheat the oven to 375°F (190°C). Grease and line a 10in (25cm) springform cake pan with parchment paper.

For the dough, sift the flour and salt together. Add ½ cup (85g) of the sugar, the egg and butter. With your hands, mix and work the ingredients together until the dough becomes smooth and pliable. On a floured surface, roll out the dough slightly larger than the diameter of the pan. Transfer the dough to the pan—there should be a rim of about 1in (3cm) around the sides.

Using baking beans, blind bake the pie crust for about 12 minutes. Remove the baking beans and leave to cool.

Meanwhile, beat the egg whites to soft peaks. Continue beating and add 1 tablespoon of the remaining 1 cup (200g) sugar at a time; beat until the sugar is completely dissolved. Continue until all the sugar has been added. If you rub some of the meringue between your thumb and index finger and you can still feel grains; the meringue will start to ooze liquid after baking.

Divide the meringue into 2 equal parts. Reserve one part, and gently fold the hazelnuts into the other part of the meringue. Then fold in the fruit and spread in the pie crust. Spread the reserved meringue over the top of the tart.

Reduce the oven temperature to 350°F (180°C) and bake for about 50 minutes. The tips of the meringue should start turning light golden, and the meringue should sound hollow when knocked gently. Leave the cake to cool in the pan.

This cake is best eaten fresh, since the meringue can get soggy when the cake is stored.

serves 12

2 CUPS (250G) ALL-PURPOSE FLOUR,
PLUS EXTRA FOR DUSTING

1 PINCH SALT

1½ CUPS (285G) SUPERFINE SUGAR

1 MEDIUM EGG

9 TABLESPOONS (125G), CUBED,
PLUS EXTRA FOR GREASING

4 MEDIUM EGG WHITES

1 CUP (100G), GROUND

18OZ (500G) RED CURRANTS
OR FROZEN SUMMER FRUIT

Birnen-Kuchen mit Guss
Pear Tart with Sour Cream

This tart combines moist, soft pears and a rich, custard-like filling with a chocolate pie crust that is not too sweet. A very satisfying and classic combination.

Preheat the oven to 425°F (220°C). Line and grease a 10in (25cm) springform cake pan with parchment paper.

For the pie dough, sift the flour, cocoa powder, and salt together. Add ½ cup (85g) of the sugar, 1 egg, and the butter. With your hands, mix and work the ingredients together until the dough becomes smooth and pliable. On a floured surface, roll out the dough slightly larger than the diameter of the pan. Transfer the pie crust to the pan—there should be a rim of about 1in (3cm) around the sides.

Using baking beans, blind bake the pie crust for about 12 minutes. Remove from the oven and reduce the temperature to 350°F (180°C).

While the pie crust is baking, peel the pears, cut them in half lengthwise, and remove the cores.

Sprinkle the crust with ground almonds. Place the eight pear halves, cut-side down, on top of the almonds. It might be necessary to trim the pears a bit.

For the filling, put the sour cream, 2 remaining eggs, the remaining sugar, and the spices into a bowl and beat until evenly distributed. Pour the filling over the pears. Do not overfill the tart—there should be no spill over the edge.

Bake the tart for about 50 minutes. The filling will still be a light color, but darker patches will start showing. Leave to cool before eating. This tart keeps in an airtight container for up to 3 days.

serves 12

1¾ CUPS (200G) ALL-PURPOSE FLOUR

⅔ CUP (50G) COCOA POWDER

1 PINCH SALT

⅔ CUP (125G) SUPERFINE SUGAR

3 MEDIUM EGGS

9 TABLESPOONS (125G), CUBED, PLUS EXTRA FOR GREASING

4 PEARS, RIPE, BUT FIRM

⅔ CUP (60G) GROUND ALMONDS

11OZ (300G) SOUR CREAM

¼ TEASPOON GROUND CARDAMOM

¼ TEASPOON GROUND NUTMEG

Apfelkuchen mit Marzipan-Guss
Apple Marzipan Tart

Marzipan has always been a favorite of mine, and this cake uses it to give a humble apple tart a rich almond flavor and a beautiful creamy texture.

serves 12

2 CUPS (250G) ALL-PURPOSE FLOUR, PLUS EXTRA FOR DUSTING

1 PINCH SALT

⅓ CUP SUPERFINE SUGAR

½ CUP (90G) STRONG VANILLA SUGAR (page 180) OR VANILLA BEAN PASTE

3 MEDIUM EGGS

9 TABLESPOONS (125G) UNSALTED BUTTER, CUBED, PLUS EXTRA FOR GREASING

2½LB (1KG) APPLES
(use apples that keep their shape when baked, e.g., Granny Smith)

3 TABLESPOONS CORNSTARCH

9OZ (250ML) WHOLE MILK

5OZ (150G) MARZIPAN
(page 189, or ready-made)

Preheat the oven to 375°F (190°C). Line and grease a 10in (25cm) springform cake pan with parchment paper.

For the pie dough, sift the flour and salt together. Add the superfine sugar, 2 teaspoons of the vanilla sugar, 1 egg, and the butter. With your hands, mix and work the ingredients together until the dough becomes smooth and pliable. On a floured surface, roll out the dough slightly larger than the diameter of the pan. Transfer the dough to the pan—there should be a rim of about 1½in (4cm) around the sides.

Peel, core, and slice the apples. The slices should be about ¼in (5mm) thick. Spread the slices over the crust.

For the filling, mix the cornstarch, remaining vanilla sugar, and some of the milk together to get a smooth, thick liquid without any lumps.

Tear the marzipan into little flakes.

Bring the remaining milk to a boil and beat in the cornstarch mixture. Continue boiling and beating for about a minute. Reduce the heat and add the marzipan. Stir until the marzipan is completely dissolved. Remove from the heat and leave to cool. Once lukewarm, beat in the remaining 2 eggs. Pour the filling over the apples and spread evenly.

Bake for about 50 minutes. The filling might get some variation in color, depending on the distribution of the apples.

Leave the cake to cool for 30 minutes, then remove from the pan to cool completely. This cake is best on the second day, and it keeps for 3–4 days in an airtight container.

serves 12

2 CUPS (240G) ALL-PURPOSE FLOUR,
PLUS EXTRA FOR DUSTING

¼ CUP (20G) COCOA POWDER

⅞ CUP/14 TABLESPOONS (200G)
UNSALTED BUTTER, COLD, CUBED,
PLUS EXTRA FOR GREASING

⅞ CUP (175G) SUPERFINE SUGAR

2 CUPS (200G) NUTS, GROUND
(hazelnuts or almonds, with skin on)

1½ TEASPOONS GROUND CINNAMON

¼ TEASPOON GROUND CLOVES

1 MEDIUM EGG

1 TABLESPOON KIRSCH

14OZ (400G) RASPBERRY JAM

1 EGG YOLK FOR GLAZING

CONFECTIONERS' SUGAR FOR DUSTING

Linzer Torte

Every year, at the end of November, the Christmas baking season was kickstarted in our house by making Linzer Torte. The small kitchen filled with the smell of cinnamon, cloves, kirsch, and freshly ground nuts. My brother and I were always heavily involved. Under our mother's direction, we measured the ingredients, ground the nuts, and made the dough. This is the best-tasting raw dough you can get!

The usual technique for making this dough was a bit intimidating to me: the flour, cocoa powder, spices, nuts, and sugar are piled on the table, the butter cubes are sprinkled on top. Then a well is made in which the egg and the kirsch go. Using a big chef's knife, the mountain is then repeatedly cut and re-erected. It is a huge credit to my mother that she taught us this method and we never came to harm.

This recipe can be made with the usual, less dangerous, all-in-one method, which I recommend below. This version of Linzer Torte unfolds its full flavor after a couple of weeks in an airtight container.

Put all the ingredients, except the jam, egg yolk, and confectioners' sugar, into a big bowl. Mix and knead swiftly with your hands until the dough holds together well. Make a ball, wrap in plastic wrap and let it rest in the fridge for at least 2 hours.

Once the dough has rested, preheat the oven to 375°F (190°C). Grease a 10in (25cm) springform or sandwich pan.

Reserve one-third of the dough for decorations. On a lightly floured surface, roll out two-thirds of the dough until about ½in (1cm) thick and slightly bigger than the pan. Transfer the dough to the pan. The dough is quite brittle, and tears are not unusual. Make sure there is a rim all the way round, about ¾in (2cm) high. You can cut any excess and use it to patch up the rim in other places. Prick the bottom of the cake with a fork.

Apply some decoration to the rim. I use two forks, one in each hand, with the rounded sides facing each other, grab a 1in (3cm) stretch of the rim and squeeze it between the forks. Repeat all the way around the rim.

Fill the cake with jam—you should have an even layer, about ¼in (4mm) thick.

Roll out the remaining one-third of the dough until about ¼in (4mm) thick for the decorations. If you want to make the classic lattice pattern, cut the dough into strips and place them on the jam. You can also decorate the cake with star or leaf patterns or other geometric ideas. Using a brush, glaze the decorations and rim with the egg yolk, trying not to get egg yolk onto the jam.

Bake for 30–40 minutes; watch the color of the rim and the egg yolk—the color of the rim should be brown, like milk chocolate.

Leave to cool for about 10 minutes, then remove from the pan and let cool on a wire rack. Dust with confectioners' sugar to serve.

This cake tastes great fresh, but it improves greatly over time, stored in an airtight container in a cool place.

Marmor-Kuchen
Marble Cake

This cake was a standard on our Sunday morning table and has a lot of nostalgia for me. It is quick to make, moist and flavorful, and the marble pattern was always fascinating to me as a child.

serves 12–24, depending on pan size. The amounts given are for a 2lb (950g) loaf pan or a Bundt pan. For a bigger Bundt pan, double the amounts and bake for 15 minutes longer.

FOR THE BATTER

9 TABLESPOONS (125G) UNSALTED BUTTER OR MARGARINE, ROOM TEMPERATURE

2 TEASPOONS VANILLA EXTRACT

2 EGGS, SEPARATED

⅞ CUP (180G) SUPERFINE SUGAR

2 CUPS (250G) ALL-PURPOSE FLOUR

1¾ TEASPOONS BAKING POWDER

½ CUP (125ML) WHOLE MILK

FOR THE CHOCOLATE BATTER

2 TABLESPOONS COCOA POWDER

3 TEASPOONS SUPERFINE SUGAR

2 TABLESPOONS HEAVY CREAM

¼ TEASPOON GROUND CLOVES

Preheat the oven to 350°F (180°C).

Put the butter in a bowl and, using a hand mixer or a stand mixer fitted with the balloon whisk, beat the butter until it is light and pale. Add the vanilla extract and egg yolks, alternating with the sugar bit by bit, and beat for another 15 minutes, until the butter and sugar mix is very frothy and white.

Sift the flour and baking powder together in a bowl. Alternate adding the flour and milk bit by bit to the batter while beating on a low speed.

In a separate bowl, beat the egg whites to soft peaks. Fold the egg whites into the butter and flour mixture.

For the chocolate batter, take one-third of the plain batter and put it into a separate bowl. Fold in the ingredients for the chocolate batter.

Put the two batters in a greased 2lb (950g) Bundt pan or a loaf pan, starting with the vanilla batter, then add a layer of chocolate batter and finish with vanilla batter. Use a fork to create the marble effect by pulling it through the layers of batter with a swirling motion.

Bake for about 1 hour; the cake should start separating from the pan and a skewer inserted into the cake should come out clean. Cover with foil if the top of the cake starts getting too dark.

Leave the cake to cool in the pan for at least 20 minutes before attempting to take it out of the pan.

This cake keeps very well for up to a week in an airtight container and for the first 3 days its flavor actually improves.

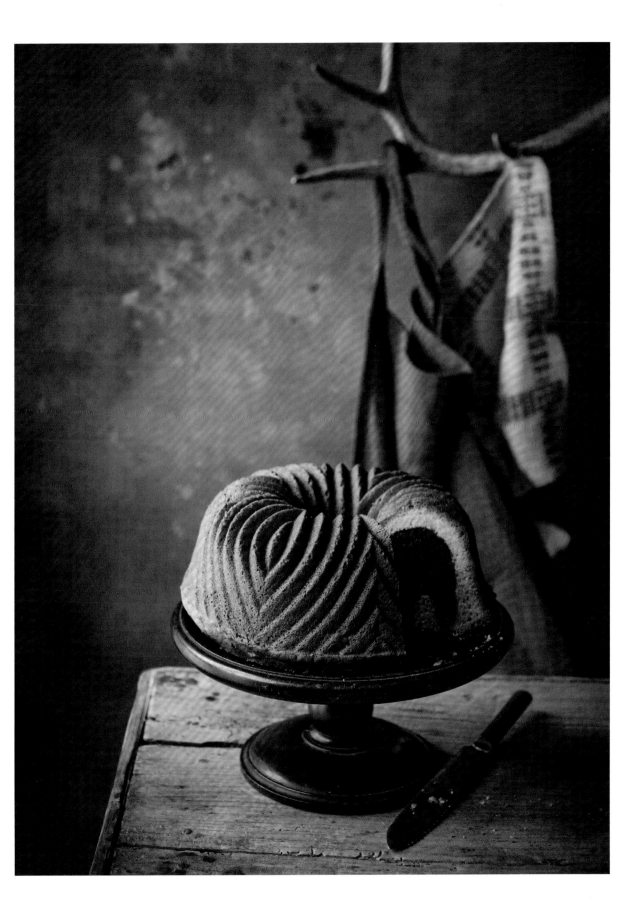

Zitronenkuchen
Lemon Cake

serves 10

4 MEDIUM EGGS, SEPARATED

9 TABLESPOONS (125G) UNSALTED BUTTER, ROOM TEMPERATURE

9 TABLESPOONS (125G) MARGARINE, ROOM TEMPERATURE

⅞ CUP (175G) SUPERFINE SUGAR

2 TEASPOONS VANILLA SUGAR (PAGE 180)

1⅞ CUPS (225G) ALL-PURPOSE FLOUR OR WHITE SPELT FLOUR, SIFTED

⅔ CUP (75G) CORNSTARCH

1 PINCH SALT

LEMON ZEST FROM 1 LEMON

3 TABLESPOONS LEMON JUICE

3½ TEASPOONS BAKING POWDER

½ TEASPOON LEMON EXTRACT

FOR THE ICING
1¼ CUPS (125G)
CONFECTIONERS' SUGAR, SIFTED

4 TEASPOONS LEMON JUICE

I always loved lemon cake—it can be whisked up very quickly and is always satisfying to have with a cup of coffee. This sponge cake is different from the usual lemon drizzle cake, and it should be moist, despite not being soaked in lemon juice. The recipe uses a substantial amount of cornstarch, and the remaining flour can be substituted with white spelt flour.

Preheat the oven to 375°F (190°C). Prepare a 2lb (950g) loaf pan by lining with parchment paper.

Beat the egg whites to soft peaks.

Put the butter, margarine, sugar, and vanilla sugar in a bowl and beat with a hand mixer, or with a stand mixer fitted with the balloon whisk, until frothy and light. Keep beating and add the egg yolks one by one. Stir in the sifted flour, cornstarch, salt, lemon zest and juice, and lemon extract. Fold in the egg whites. Transfer the batter to the prepared pan.

Bake for about 45 minutes, being careful not to overbake. A skewer inserted into the center should come out clean. Leave to cool in the pan for about 10 minutes, then turn the cake onto a wire rack.

For the icing, combine the confectioners' sugar and lemon juice—it should be fairly runny. Spread the icing on the warm cake and let cool completely. The cake will taste best on the second day, but will keep for 5 days stored in an airtight container.

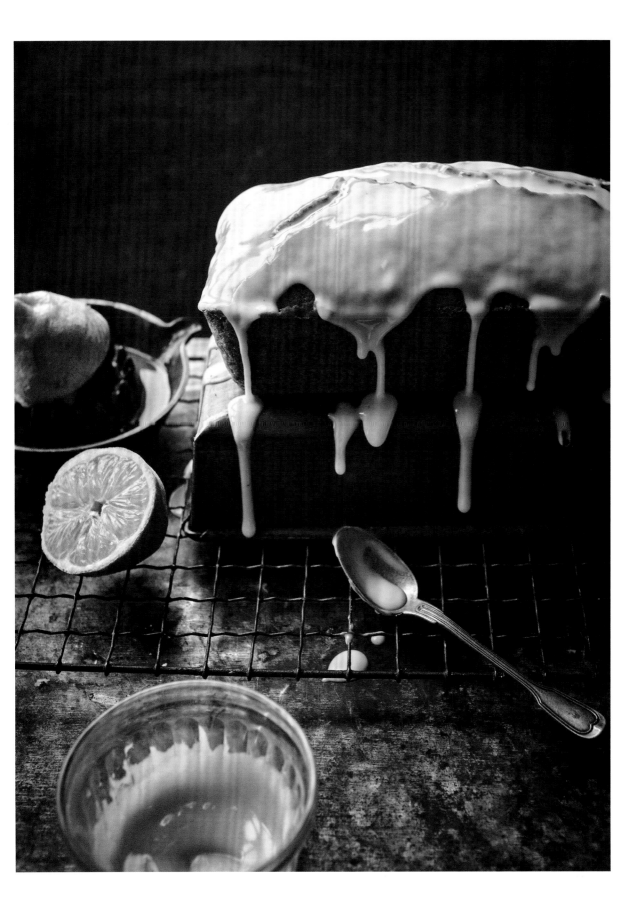

Obstkuchen
Fruit Sponge Cake

serves 12

1½ TABLESPOONS UNSALTED BUTTER,
PLUS EXTRA FOR GREASING

⅓ CUP (80G) SUPERFINE SUGAR

2 MEDIUM EGGS

½ CUP (60G) ALL-PURPOSE FLOUR

½ PORTION VANILLA PUDDING
(page 184), COOLED

FRESH FRUIT (no pineapples or kiwi!)

9OZ (250ML) WATER OR CLEAR FRUIT JUICE

1½ TEASPOONS AGAR-AGAR FLAKES

When we were in a hurry to get a cake ready, this was often the cake of choice. My mother would send my brother or me to the shop next door to buy a ready-made sponge cake. Then we were all involved cutting up fruit and making the gelatin glaze. Sometimes we would also make a custard, as in this recipe, which stops the fruit juice from soaking into the sponge cake.

Laying out the fruit in nice patterns was always fun for us kids, and this cake is a great treat on a hot summer afternoon.

A note about the pan: In Germany there are pans for this, which look like flan pans, with a raised center, so when you turn the baked sponge cake upside down you have a nice, fluted rim. The fruit sits in that large indentation, which helps to contain the glaze as well. If you don't have this type of pan, a flan pan or sandwich pan will also work well.

The sponge cake can be baked the day before.

Preheat the oven to 375°F (190°C). Grease a 10in (25cm) flan or sandwich pan.

Melt the butter—it should be liquid, but not hot.

Put three-quarters of the sugar and the eggs into a big heatproof bowl and beat over boiling water until frothy and a temperature of 110°F (43°C) is reached. Take off the heat and continue beating until the mixture is cold and a bit stiffer.

Fold in the flour, then fold in the melted butter. Transfer the batter into the pan and spread evenly, taking care not to handle the batter too much.

Bake for about 12 minutes. The sponge cake should separate from the pan and be golden in color. Turn onto a wire rack and leave to cool.

Spread the cooled vanilla custard evenly over the sponge cake.

Clean the fruit and cut it into bite-sized chunks, if desired. Arrange the fruit on top.

For the glaze, put the water or fruit juice and remaining sugar into a saucepan. Sprinkle the agar-agar flakes on top. Bring the glaze gently to a boil, stirring occasionally. Once all the agar-agar flakes are dissolved, remove the saucepan from the heat.

Let the glaze cool a bit before coating the fruit on the tart. Leave the glaze to cool and set. Due to the fresh fruit, this cake should be eaten within 1 day.

MY COUSINS WITH MY GRANDMOTHER AND ME. SHE ALWAYS HAD SOME PASTRIES OR ROLLS FOR US, AND SHE LOVED TO ORGANIZE BARBECUES AND SUMMER PARTIES IN THE GARDEN.

Sweet and savory breads and rolls

*T*he reason I started baking in earnest was my longing for German bread. Almost by chance I found the book *Bread Matters* by Andrew Whitley, which got me going. My son's primary school, with its regular fairs and community gatherings, gave me plenty of opportunities to expand my skills.

I was always intrigued by yeasted doughs and sourdough, and, after some research, I I managed to make bread that looked and tasted just as I wanted. But there were also sweet breads, such as brioche and diverse braids, and the other German yeasted baked goods: my quest for bread opened a whole food universe for me.

In this chapter, I am sharing some baked goods I enjoyed while I lived in Germany, and that are usually bought from a bakery, as well as some sweet breads we baked at home.

Schwäbische Seele
Swabian Spelt Rolls

On my regular commute to London, I always used to sit in the same area of a specific railroad car, as did many of the other commuters. For a couple of years, there were three of us software developers at the same table. We got to talking, and it appeared the other two were foodies, one of them having worked as a chef. We soon started regular breakfasts on the train once a week; the other two brought cheese and cold cuts, while I treated them to a variety of breads!

This, of course, got noticed by other commuters, and one of them told me of the Swabian Seele (meaning "soul") he was missing from his time in Ravensburg. They are made with spelt flour, using a very wet, soft dough and a long, slow process. Typically, they are topped with caraway seeds and rock salt. After some research, I came up with this recipe, using a pâte fermentée, which is a yeasted, salted starter.

makes 6

FOR THE STARTER
1¼ CUPS (160G) WHITE SPELT FLOUR

½ CUP (130ML) WATER

½ TEASPOON INSTANT YEAST

½ TEASPOON SALT

FOR THE DOUGH
2 CUPS (260G) WHITE SPELT FLOUR

1¼ CUPS (140G) BREAD FLOUR

1½ TEASPOONS SALT

½ TEASPOON INSTANT YEAST

1¼ CUPS (300ML) WATER

CARAWAY SEEDS
FOR SPRINKLING

ROCK SALT CRYSTALS,
FOR SPRINKLING

VEGETABLE OIL,
FOR GREASING

On the day before baking, put all the starter ingredients in a bowl and mix them well. Cover and leave to stand at room temperature for about 2 hours. Then put the starter into the fridge overnight, until it is needed.

On baking day, put the flours, salt, and yeast in a bowl and mix to disperse the ingredients. Add the water and all of the starter and mix until all is well incorporated. Knead the dough until the gluten is very well developed. In a stand mixer fitted with a dough hook this can take up to 20 minutes. Check that it is ready using the windowpane test (see page 201)—the dough needs to be very elastic but holding together very well.

Transfer the dough to a lightly oiled bowl and leave to proof at room temperature for 2 hours, folding the dough 3 times during the first hour. The dough is ready for shaping when it feels fragile, and when touched and lightly dented, it doesn't recover its shape. There should be some big bubbles.

Since these rolls are baked directly after shaping, preheat the oven to its hottest setting well ahead of time.

continued

*It is important to be gentle when
handling this dough as it is fragile,
and when touched and lightly dented,
it doesn't recover its shape. This is why
it is "cut" with the edge of your hands.*

Line two baking pans with silicone sheets or parchment paper.

Spread some flour on the work surface to prevent the dough from sticking. Turn the dough onto the work surface and gently pull it to form a rectangle about 1in (2cm) thick. Using your hands, fingertips touching and palms facing you, cut an oval piece off the dough rectangle by cutting through the dough with your hands. With the edge of your hand on the table, pull the piece of dough toward you so that it folds a bit onto itself and forms a roll with some surface tension. Transfer the rolls to the prepared baking pan and continue until the dough is used up. The dough should yield six rolls of about 6oz (170g). Liberally spray the rolls with water and sprinkle with caraway seeds and rock salt.

Bake immediately for about 20 minutes. To get a crisp crust, spray the rolls halfway through baking.

Eat the rolls filled with BLT, cheese and lettuce, or tomato, mozzarella and basil, or any filling of your choice. These rolls should be eaten soon after baking, as the salt will attract water.

Milchbrötchen
Milk Rolls

Ever since I started breadmaking in the UK, I have wanted to replicate the milk rolls we bought in the shop next door when I lived in Germany. They got their baked goods from a traditional baker, Hermann Faisst. At a time when many bakeries adopted time-saving methods and mixes, he stuck to his craft. His milk rolls were simple and unglazed. The crust was thin, golden, covered in little bubbles, and a bit flaky. The crumb was soft and moist. They could be eaten with almost anything, but butter and honey were my favorite toppings. This recipe is as close as I have come to re-creating the original.

makes 12

4 CUPS (500G) BREAD FLOUR,
PLUS EXTRA FOR DUSTING

1½ CUPS (340ML) WHOLE MILK, COOL

2 TEASPOONS INSTANT YEAST

2 TEASPOONS SUPERFINE SUGAR

2 TEASPOONS SALT

¼ CUP (60G) UNSALTED BUTTER,
ROOM TEMPERATURE

Line two baking sheets with parchment paper or silicone sheets.

Put all the ingredients in a bowl. Use your hands or a stand mixer fitted with the dough hook to mix the ingredients thoroughly and knead until the gluten is well developed (see the windowpane test on page 201). Cover and leave to prove at room temperature for about 1 hour.

Divide the dough into 2½oz (70g) pieces. Shape these pieces into balls and place them well apart on the prepared baking sheets.

Prepare the oven for proofing—place a roasting pan in the bottom of the oven. Bring about 2 cups (500ml) water to a boil. Place the baking sheets with the dough balls in the oven. Pour the boiling water into the roasting pan and close the door. This will allow the rolls to proof in a moist, warm environment.

After 40 minutes, take the sheets out of the oven, empty the roasting pan, and put it back in the oven. Bring more water to a boil.

Take a thick skewer or a cake dowel and press it down onto each dough ball to create two halves. Press it almost all the way through to the bottom. Use a bit of flour to stop the dough from sticking to the dowel.

Put the sheets with the rolls back into the oven, pour the boiling water into the roasting pan, close the door, and proof for another 40 minutes.

Take the baking sheets and sheet pan out of the oven and preheat the oven to 450°F (230°C). Keep the rolls moist by spraying them with water. If you like, you can glaze the rolls with milk or egg wash before baking.

Once the oven is hot, put the baking sheets back in the oven and bake the rolls for 12–15 minutes, until dark golden in color. These rolls are best fresh, but can be frozen.

Butter-Hörnchen
Butter Crescents

On those Saturdays when there was no school, or during the holidays, when one of us managed to pop out to the village bakery before breakfast, these fresh butter crescents were always a special treat. Crisp on the outside, fluffy on the inside, they are best eaten by smearing butter on the end and biting it off. Nothing else needed!

makes 6

2⅓ CUPS (300G) BREAD FLOUR, PLUS EXTRA FOR DUSTING

¾ CUP (175ML) WATER, LUKEWARM

2 TEASPOONS INSTANT YEAST

2 TABLESPOONS UNSALTED BUTTER, ROOM TEMPERATURE

1 TEASPOON SALT

Put all the ingredients in a bowl and mix by hand or with a stand mixer fitted with the dough hook. Once all the ingredients are well incorporated, knead until the dough forms a smooth ball and the gluten is well developed (see the windowpane test on page 201). Cover and leave to proof at room temperature for about 1½ hours.

Once the dough has proofed, turn it onto a lightly floured surface. Divide it into 6 equal pieces weighing about 3oz (85g) each. Shape the pieces into balls and let them sit covered on the work surface for about 5 minutes, to relax the gluten.

Using a rolling pin, roll the pieces into ovals, about 6in (15cm) wide and 8in (20cm) long. If the dough gets stiff, move on to the next piece and let the gluten relax. After about 4–5 rolling cycles, you should have thin ovals of the right dimensions. It doesn't have to be exact, but the crescents are better with thinner pieces of dough.

To shape the crescents, starting at the far end, roll up a piece halfway, then stretch the rolled-up part to become about 10in (25cm) wide, and continue rolling to the end. You now have a log with a thick middle and thinner ends. Transfer the log to a lined baking sheet and repeat with the remaining ovals. (A standard 16 x 14in (40 x 35cm) baking sheet has space for 6 crescents, so make sure they sit well apart from each other.)

Cover with a dish towel or a plastic bag and proof for about 1 hour until the crescents are well risen and feel a bit fragile. Preheat the oven to 450°F (230°C).

Bake for 15–20 minutes, until the crescents are a rich golden color. These crescents are great with some butter, or a soft-boiled egg. Best eaten fresh.

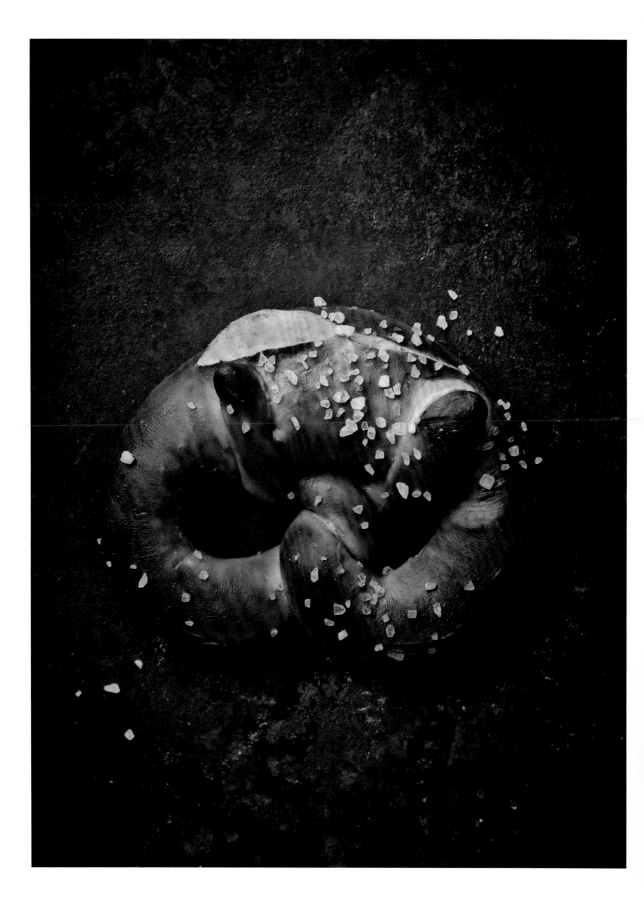

Laugen-Brezel
Soft Pretzel

Pretzels, or Brezeln or Brezn in German, are the most iconic German food. Ornaments of pretzels adorn every bakery, and images of them can be found on medieval church windows in Freiburg, where I come from. Often a pretzel works better as a soother for an upset baby than a pacifier. They are a part of my upbringing and heritage. And still, there is no better snack after a long shopping spree through my hometown of Freiburg than a Brezel from the bakery at the tram stop. There are many subtle regional differences in shaping, fat content, and the use of water, milk, or cream. Here is a standard recipe for a pretzel you could buy on Freiburg's streets.

Disclaimer about lye (German, Lauge): I am giving two options for the finish. One is using lye, which involves a very dangerous chemical, solid sodium hydroxide. The other option uses baking soda, which is bicarbonate of soda, and is not dangerous at all. The results are different in color and taste, but without a direct comparison the baking soda pretzel can stand its ground. If you intend to use lye, I'd recommend baking a few batches of pretzels with baking soda, but treat it as if it were lye, to practice the handling and have everything in the right place before starting.

makes 8–10

FOR THE STARTER
1 CUP (100G) BREAD FLOUR

½ TEASPOON SALT

⅛ TEASPOON INSTANT YEAST

¼ CUP (65ML) WATER

FOR THE DOUGH
3½ CUPS (400G) BREAD FLOUR

2 TEASPOONS SALT

1 TABLESPOON HONEY

1¾ TEASPOONS INSTANT YEAST

2 TABLESPOONS UNSALTED BUTTER,
ROOM TEMPERATURE

6OZ (180ML) WATER

COARSE SALT CRYSTALS,
FOR SPRINKLING

FOR THE LYE OR BICARB DIPPING SOLUTION
8 CUPS (2 LITERS) WATER

1½ TEASPOONS SALT

⅓ CUP (80G) BAKING SODA
or ⅓ CUP (80G) SODIUM HYDROXIDE PELLETS

Prepare the starter the day before baking. Combine all the ingredients in a bowl and mix with your hand or a spatula until all the flour is incorporated. Cover with plastic wrap and leave to stand at room temperature for about 2 hours. Then put the starter in the fridge overnight until you need it—it will be good to use for up to 3 days.

About 1 hour before making the main dough, take the starter out of the fridge.

To make the main dough, combine all the ingredients except the salt crystals and the starter in a bowl and mix with your hand or a spatula. The resulting dough will be very stiff. Knead the dough on a work surface for about 10 minutes. Don't use any additional flour; you won't need it anyway. The resulting dough should be smooth and a bit elastic. Put the dough into a bowl, cover, and proof at room temperature for about 2 hours. Fold the dough once after 1 hour.

continued

Meanwhile, prepare the dipping solution. Use a big stainless-steel pan and stainless-steel spoons for dipping. Cover your normal work surfaces in case lye spills. When dipping, keep the baking sheets very close to the lye pan and the oven. Always wear protective gloves and goggles when working with sodium hydroxide and lye. Never ever touch sodium hydroxide pellets with your skin.

If using baking soda, bring the water to a boil. Switch off the heat, add the salt, and stir. Then add the baking soda—there will be a bit of frothing and splashing, so be careful. Leave to cool.

If using sodium hydroxide, put the water in the pan and then add the sodium hydroxide pellets. Sodium hydroxide creates a lot of heat when it dissolves.

Once the dough has proofed, divide it into pieces weighing 3oz (85g) each. Roll each piece of dough into a cylinder. Once all the pieces have been rolled, start again with the first piece, to roll it into a long strand with thin ends and a belly in the middle. Aim for a length of 24in (60cm). Make sure you don't tear your strands—if there is too much resistance in the dough, move on to the next strand. You will need several cycles to reach the length required.

Now shape the pretzels—the bakers use a slinging method, but there is a simpler, slower way to do this (see photos). Make sure the ends of the little arms are well attached to the middle part.

Place the pretzels onto lined baking sheets, cover, and leave to proof at room temperature for about 45 minutes. Uncover the pretzels and put them in the fridge for 30 minutes, so that a skin can form.

Preheat the oven to 475°F (245°C).

Take the pretzels out of the fridge. Dip each pretzel in lye or sodium carbonate solution for about 5 seconds. Transfer the pretzel back onto the lined baking sheet. One sheet will hold 4–5 pretzels. Once the sheet is full, slash the thickest part of the pretzels with a sharp serrated knife and sprinkle with salt crystals. Transfer to the oven immediately and bake for 12–15 minutes. Leave to cool on a wire rack. Repeat with the remaining pretzels.

Because of the salt, these pretzels are best eaten fresh.

Flammkuchen
Flame Cake

serves 6

FOR THE DOUGH
4 CUPS (500G) BREAD FLOUR

2½OZ (75ML) VEGETABLE OIL

1¼ CUPS (300ML) WATER WATER

1 TEASPOON SALT

FOR THE TOPPINGS
CRÈME FRAÎCHE
OR SOUR CREAM, AS NEEDED

SALT, AS NEEDED

GROUND NUTMEG, AS NEEDED

BLACK PEPPER, GROUND, AS NEEDED

RED ONIONS, THINLY SLICED, AS NEEDED

BACON CUBES, AS NEEDED

CINNAMON SUGAR, AS NEEDED
(page 181, for sweet toppings)

APPLE SLICES, AS NEEDED
(for sweet toppings)

For some time during my years at university, I played music with a teacher from the Ortenau area, near Offenburg and Strasburg. She often organized courses, and on one of those music courses we all went to a country pub. I learned that Flammkuchen was in season. In the area, Flammkuchen used to be only served through the time of the wine harvest. The pubs were booked weeks in advance. And once you arrived at the pub, you ordered by the square meter!

The crisp base, in combination with the simple toppings, is an incredibly sensuous match, and it is no wonder that Flammkuchen or tarte flambée is now almost universally available. There are lots of recipes out there using pizza dough and different bread doughs. Other recipes that claim to be original Alsatian (Ortenau and Alsace are only divided by the Rhine River and have a lot of similarities) use unleavened dough, and this fact makes Flammkuchen incredibly quick to make.

Mix all of the dough ingredients until well combined. Knead the dough until a smooth ball forms. Leave the dough to rest at least 15 minutes before using it. Preheat the oven to the highest temperature possible, using a pizza stone if you have one.

Divide the dough into portions weighing 5½oz (150g) each. Roll each portion as thinly as possible—if the dough starts to pull back and gets unwieldy, let it rest for a few minutes and move on to the next one.

Transfer the flammkuchen onto a piece of parchment paper (you can do the last rolling step on parchment paper, to avoid tearing). Cover the flammkuchen base thinly with crème fraîche or sour cream and add your topping of choice. The classic is lardons and onions, with a seasoning of nutmeg, black pepper, and salt, but plain sour cream with nutmeg is also very tasty. For a sweet variant, try a sprinkle of cinnamon sugar and thin apple slices.

Bake the flammkuchen for about 10 minutes in a domestic oven, or 2 minutes in a pizza oven, until they are getting crisp around the edge. They need to be eaten immediately. The dough can be stored in an airtight container in the fridge for several days.

serves 12

4 CUPS (500G) BREAD FLOUR

¼ CUP (50G) SUPERFINE SUGAR

3 MEDIUM EGGS

1 CUP (225ML) WHOLE MILK

2 TEASPOONS SALT

1 X ¼OZ (7G) PACKET INSTANT YEAST,
OR 2½ TEASPOONS

¾ CUP (175G) UNSALTED BUTTER, CUBED,
AT ROOM TEMPERATURE,
PLUS EXTRA FOR GREASING

3½OZ (100G) RAISINS, ABOUT ⅔ CUP RAISINS

FLAKED ALMONDS
OR BLANCHED ALMONDS, AS NEEDED

CONFECTIONERS' SUGAR FOR DUSTING

Gugelhupf

This cake has a very long tradition in Austria, Eastern Europe, France, and Germany. The name is possibly derived from the name of a monk's hood. The first printed recipe is in Marx Rumpoldt's cookbook from 1591. There are lots of different spellings, and even more regional traditions when it comes to flavors. But all Gugelhupf cakes have two things in common: first, the mold, a Bundt pan with a specific pattern and a spike in the middle, and second, the base, which is a highly enriched yeasted dough that is very soft.

The Alsace, just across the Rhine River opposite the Black Forest, is one of the regions where Gugelhupf is a local specialty, baked in a Bundt pan made of clay. Usually, this variant is not strongly flavored and not very sweet, but incredibly delicious. After a long Sunday family walk, it can't get much better than having a slice of Gugelhupf with butter and a cup of coffee!

This dough will be very soft, so a stand mixer with kneading hook is recommended. But, it is possible, with patience and stamina, to mix and knead this by hand.

Put the flour, sugar, eggs, milk, salt, and yeast in a bowl. Mix and knead until the gluten is well formed. This dough is too slack to ever form a ball, but what you are looking for is a change in texture and shine. The dough will be a bit less sticky. This will take about 10 minutes in a stand mixer fitted with the dough hook. Doing this by hand might take longer, depending on your technique.

Add the butter and continue kneading until the butter is completely integrated. This is the hardest part when hand kneading, but be assured that it will happen, and the result is worth it. Put the dough back into the bowl if kneading on a surface, cover and leave to proof at room temperature for 1–1½ hours.

Add the raisins and work them into the dough, using a spatula.

Grease a 9in (23cm) diameter Bundt pan with butter. Line the bottom of the pan with flaked or blanched almonds (one in every groove). Transfer the dough to the pan, cover and leave to proof at room temperature for an hour.

Preheat the oven to 350°F (180°C).

Bake the gugelhupf for 40–50 minutes, depending on the pan you are using, since different pans vary considerably in their heat absorption. The cake should be dark golden-brown. Cover with foil if it is getting too dark to prevent it from browning further.

Leave to cool in the pan for about 30 minutes, then remove from the pan to cool completely.

Dust liberally with confectioners' sugar. Gugelhupf is best eaten within a day of baking.

Hefezopf
Yeasted Braid

"Yeasted braid," or Hefezopf in German, is a classic that comes in all different shapes and sizes. It is probably the food that best exemplifies the fluidity of cultures and national borders in the European past (Great Britain excluded). The two defining words say it all—yeast and braid. They can be very simple, just a glazed braided, lightly enriched loaf, or a heavily filled braid made with spiced brioche dough. All sorts of variations exist, which are often local specialties. You will find Hefezopf and its variations in other countries under different names, such as babka, challah, or couronne.

Schweizer Sonntags Zopf
Swiss Sunday Braid

I came to appreciate the Swiss Sunday braid on my frequent visits to Switzerland. This fluffy bread is like the milk rolls (see page 98), but doesn't contain any sugar, which it a very versatile companion for all sorts of sweet and savory toppings. Swiss bakers use a specific flour for this that is called Zopfmehl, meaning "braid flour." It is a mix of bread flour and white spelt flour, which gives the dough ideal characteristics for braiding, and will result in a close, but fluffy texture. The spelt flour can be replaced with all-purpose, if you wish.

Put both flours, the salt, and yeast into a bowl and mix briefly. Add the remaining ingredients, except the egg. Using your hands or a stand mixer fitted with the dough hook, mix the ingredients until the butter and liquids are well incorporated. Knead until a smooth ball forms and the gluten is well developed (see the windowpane test on page 201). Cover and leave to proof at room temperature for about 1 hour.

Once the dough has proofed, divide the dough and braid it to your liking; three-strand braids are classic for this bread. Cover your braid with a plastic bag or a linen dish towel and proof for about 50 minutes. The braid should be well risen and a bit jiggly.

Preheat the oven to 375°F (190°C).

Glaze the braid with beaten egg and let it sit uncovered for another 10 minutes. Glaze it again, then bake for about 30 minutes, turning the braid halfway through the bake, until golden brown. Store like bread for several days, and toast if it becomes stale.

serves 4–6

3¼ CUPS (400G) BREAD FLOUR

⅞ CUP (100G) ALL-PURPOSE FLOUR

2 TEASPOONS SALT

1¾ TEASPOONS INSTANT YEAST

⅔ CUP (150ML) WHOLE MILK, LUKEWARM

⅔ CUP (150ML) WATER, LUKEWARM

¼ CUP (60G) UNSALTED BUTTER,
AT ROOM TEMPERATURE

1 EGG, BEATEN, FOR GLAZING

Babka
Chocolate Braid

What looks more stunning than the randomly swirling bands of dark chocolate in this loaf of white, sweet bread! This style of braiding is known in many countries, and is used with different fillings as well. Always an eye catcher, it used to be a special treat on our Saturday afternoon table. The rich spices and citrus zest in combination with chocolate make this truly a great braid for any special occasion.

For the dough, put all the ingredients in a bowl and, using your hands or a stand mixer fitted with the dough hook, mix the ingredients until evenly distributed. Then knead the dough for several minutes until it has a smooth and silky texture. Cover with a dish towel or a plastic bag and leave to proof at room temperature for about 1 hour. Check with the poke test that the dough is ready (see page 201).

Meanwhile, prepare the filling. Put the chocolate, butter, and sugar into a pan and melt over low heat. Once liquid, take the pan off the heat and add the cinnamon, cloves, and cocoa powder. It's okay if the filling looks grainy.

Line a 2lb (950g) loaf pan with parchment paper.

On a lightly floured surface, roll out the dough to a rectangle measuring about 20 x 12in. Spread the chocolate filling over the dough rectangle, leaving 1in (2cm) of the far short edge uncovered. Roll up the dough rectangle, starting at the near short edge. Seal the seam by pinching it.

Place the roll on a work surface with the seam facing down and, with a sharp knife, cut the roll lengthwise into halves. Twist the halves together to form a rope. You can do this starting at one end and twist this half of the roll, and then do the same for the other half; this way you don't have to manipulate the whole length at once.

continued

serves 15

FOR THE DOUGH
1½ CUPS (190G) BREAD FLOUR

1 CUP + 2 TABLESPOONS (140G)
WHITE SPELT FLOUR OR ALL-PURPOSE FLOUR,
PLUS EXTRA FOR DUSTING

2 TEASPOONS INSTANT YEAST

1 PINCH SALT

3 TABLESPOONS SUPERFINE SUGAR

¾ CUP (180ML) WHOLE MILK

1 MEDIUM EGG

3 TABLESPOONS UNSALTED BUTTER, SOFTENED

ZEST OF 1 LEMON

ZEST OF 1 ORANGE

½ TEASPOON GROUND CARDAMOM

FOR THE FILLING
3½OZ (100G) DARK CHOCOLATE
(54% or 70% cocoa solids, to taste)

¼ CUP (60G) UNSALTED BUTTER

¼ CUP (60G) LIGHT BROWN SUGAR,
FIRMLY PACKED

2 TEASPOONS GROUND CINNAMON

½ TEASPOON GROUND CLOVES

⅓ CUP (30G) COCOA POWDER

UNSALTED BUTTER, MELTED,
OR APRICOT JAM FOR GLAZING

Place your hands palm-down on the ends and, with a scooping movement, bring the ends to meet underneath the middle of your rope. Transfer this into the lined pan, and cover with a dish towel or a plastic bag. Leave to proof for 30 minutes–1 hour until the Babka is well risen and the dough starts to feel fragile; a gentle touch with a finger will leave a dent that only slowly recovers.

Preheat the oven to 350°F (180°C).

Bake the Babka for 30–40 minutes.

Melt the butter for glazing or heat the apricot jam with a teaspoon of water. Brush the Babka with melted butter or jam as soon as it is out of the oven. Leave to cool for about 15 minutes, then carefully remove from the pan and parchment paper.

Let the Babka cool completely before eating. Stored in an airtight container it will last for 3 days.

Rosinen-Zopf
Cinnamon and Raisin Braid

serves 10

FOR THE DOUGH
1½ CUPS (190G) BREAD FLOUR

1 CUP + 2 TABLESPOONS (140G)
WHITE SPELT FLOUR OR ALL-PURPOSE FLOUR,
PLUS EXTRA FOR DUSTING

2 TEASPOONS YEAST

1 PINCH SALT

3 TABLESPOONS SUPERFINE SUGAR

¾ CUP (180ML) WHOLE MILK

1 MEDIUM EGG

3 TABLESPOONS UNSALTED BUTTER,
SOFTENED

FOR THE FILLING
7 TABLESPOONS UNSALTED BUTTER,
MELTED

CINNAMON SUGAR (page 181),
as needed (about ½ cup [100g])

RAISINS, AS NEEDED
(about 6OZ [170G], OR 1 CUP)

WALNUT PIECES, AS NEEDED
(about 4OZ [120G], ABOUT 1 CUP)

FLAKED ALMONDS (optional) FOR TOPPING

1 MEDIUM EGG, BEATEN

Cinnamon, sugar, and raisins are a classic combination. With this filling, the braid slices very well, and it won't fall apart when spread with some butter.

For the dough, put all the ingredients in a bowl and, using your hands or a stand mixer fitted with the dough hook, mix until evenly distributed. Then knead the dough for several minutes until smooth and silky. Cover with a dish towel or a plastic bag and leave to proof at room temperature for about 1 hour. Check with the poke test that the dough is ready (see page 201).

Divide the dough into three equal pieces. Dust a work surface very lightly with flour. Using a rolling pin, roll out each piece of dough to a rectangle about 16 x 8 in (40 x 20cm). This might be easier if you shape the three dough pieces into long rolls first. If the dough gets too stiff, just wait a few minutes to let the gluten relax and then continue where you left off.

Brush each rectangle with melted butter, leaving a 1in (2cm) edge along one long side of each piece uncovered. Liberally sprinkle cinnamon sugar, raisins, and walnut pieces over the buttered area. Gently press them into the dough, but not right through the dough.

Roll up each rectangle from the long side opposite the free edge into a log and seal, by slightly pressing the uncovered edge into the log. You should have three similar logs about 16in (40cm) long. Lay them out next to each other. Braid into a three-strand braid and seal the ends by flattening them a bit and tucking underneath the braid. Transfer to a lined baking sheet, cover and leave to proof for 1–1½ hours.

Preheat the oven to 350°F (180°C).

The braid should be well risen and a bit jiggly. Once the braid is ready, glaze with beaten egg and sprinkle with flaked almonds, if desired. Bake for 40 minutes. Leave to cool before eating. Stored in an airtight container, this will keep for up to 5 days. Gently toast when stale. Shown on pages 113–114.

Mohn-Zopf
Poppy Seed Braid

The poppy seeds in this braid provide some extra texture.

For the dough, put all the ingredients in a bowl and, using your hands or a stand mixer fitted with the dough hook, mix until evenly distributed. Then knead the dough for several minutes until smooth and silky. Cover with a dish towel or a plastic bag and leave to proof at room temperature for about 1 hour. Check with the poke test that the dough is ready (see page 201).

Meanwhile, prepare the filling. Peel, core, and dice the apple; the pieces should be the size of a raisin. Put the poppy seeds in a blender and blend until they have the texture of coarse semolina. Put the ground poppy seeds, sugar, lemon zest, and water into a saucepan and boil over a gentle heat, stirring constantly for about 10 minutes. If the poppy filling gets too thick and threatens to burn, add a little more water. The final consistency should be a thick, grainy mash. Take off the heat and stir in the honey and marmalade.

On a lightly floured surface, roll out the dough to a rectangle measuring about 20 x 12in (50 x 30cm). Spread the poppy seed filling over the dough rectangle, leaving 1in (2cm) of the far short edge uncovered. Sprinkle the apple pieces over the poppy filling.

Roll up the dough rectangle, starting at the nearest short edge. Seal the seam by pinching it. Place the roll on a lined baking sheet with the seam down and, with a sharp knife, cut the roll lengthwise into halves. Twist the halves together to form a rope. Pinch the ends and tuck them slightly under the rope to avoid unraveling.

Cover with a dish towel or a plastic bag and leave to proof for about 1 hour. The braid should be well risen, and the dough should feel fragile; a gentle touch will leave a dent that only slowly recovers.

Preheat the oven to 375°F (190°C). Bake the braid for about 40 minutes. Brush with melted butter while still hot.

Mix confectioners' sugar and water as required to get a medium-thick icing. Drizzle over the braid once the braid is cool. Store in an airtight container for up to 3 days.

serves 10

FOR THE DOUGH
1½ CUPS (190G) BREAD FLOUR

1 CUP + 2 TABLESPOONS (140G) WHITE SPELT FLOUR OR ALL-PURPOSE FLOUR, PLUS EXTRA FOR DUSTING

2 TEASPOONS INSTANT YEAST

1 PINCH SALT

3 TABLESPOONS SUPERFINE SUGAR

¾ CUP (180ML) WHOLE MILK

1 MEDIUM EGG

3 TABLESPOONS UNSALTED BUTTER, SOFTENED

1 TEASPOON GROUND CARDAMOM

FOR THE FILLING
1 APPLE (sour, if you like)

1¼ CUPS (175G) POPPY SEEDS

⅓ CUP (80G) SUPERFINE SUGAR

ZEST OF 1 LEMON

3OZ (100ML) WATER, PLUS EXTRA, AS NEEDED

2 TABLESPOONS HONEY

2 TABLESPOONS ORANGE MARMALADE

UNSALTED BUTTER, MELTED, FOR GLAZING

⅞ CUP (100G) CONFECTIONERS' SUGAR

Zwiebel-Zopf mit Mohn
Onion and Poppy Seed Braid

serves 15

FOR THE DOUGH
3½ CUPS (400G) BREAD FLOUR

⅞ CUP (100G) WHITE SPELT FLOUR OR ALL-PURPOSE FLOUR, PLUS EXTRA FOR DUSTING

2 TEASPOONS SALT

1¾ TEASPOONS INSTANT YEAST

1¼ CUPS (300ML) BEER OR WATER, COLD

¼ CUP (60G) UNSALTED BUTTER, ROOM TEMPERATURE

1 MEDIUM EGG

ONION SEEDS (optional) FOR SPRINKLING

FOR THE FILLING
1 TEASPOON BUTTER

10OZ (300G) ONION, FINELY CHOPPED

2 TABLESPOONS POPPY SEEDS

½ TEASPOON SALT

2 TABLESPOONS DRIED BREAD CRUMBS

This is a savory braid. I got the idea for creating this when I was thinking about some of my favorite savory filled breads and I wondered what a savory babka would look like. I loved onion-filled bread as a teenager, and more recently I discovered poppy and onion fillings that are used in Jewish rolls, such as bialys. This braid never lasts long enough in our household to get stale.

For the dough, put both flours, the salt, and yeast in a bowl and mix briefly. Add beer or water, and butter. Using your hands or a stand mixer fitted with the dough hook, mix the ingredients until the butter and liquids are well incorporated, then knead until a smooth ball forms and the gluten is well developed. Cover the dough with a dish towel or plastic bag and leave to proof at room temperature for about 1½ hours.

For the filling, in a frying pan, heat the butter, add the onions, and sauté for 5 minutes on low to medium heat until they become translucent. Transfer the onions to a bowl and add the poppy seeds, salt, and bread crumbs. Mix well and set aside to cool. The bread crumbs will soak up excess liquid from the onions during baking.

Once the dough is ready, divide it into three equal pieces. Dust a work surface very lightly with flour. Using a rolling pin, roll out each piece of dough into a rectangle about 16 x 8in (40 x 20cm). This might be easier if you shape the three dough pieces into long rolls. If the dough gets too stiff, just wait a few minutes to let the gluten relax and then continue where you left off.

Spread the filling equally over the three rectangles, leaving a 1in (2cm) edge along one long side of each piece uncovered. Next, roll up each rectangle from the long side opposite the free edge into a log, and seal by slightly pressing the uncovered edge into the log. You should have three similar logs about 16in (40cm) long.

Lay them out next to each other. Braid them into a three-strand braid and seal the ends by flattening them a bit and tugging them underneath the braid. Transfer to a lined baking sheet, cover, and leave to proof for about 1½ hours.

Preheat the oven to 375°F (190°C).

The braid should be well risen and a bit jiggly. Once the braid is ready, glaze with beaten egg and sprinkle with onion seeds, if desired.

Bake for 35 minutes. Leave to cool before eating. Store in an airtight container for up to 3 days.

Rosinen-Schnecken
Raisin Swirls

The store next door to our house in Germany sold the very best raisin swirls. The store owner was an apprentice with Hermann Faisst in his youth, the baker who made most of the bread and baked goods that were sold there, and who grew up with. I am not sure I am doing him justice with my recipe, but it comes close. The swirls were flatter than Chelsea buns and had a greater diameter. And they weren't as sweet. I loved unraveling the swirl and eating it bit by bit.

makes about 16

1 PORTION BASIC YEASTED SWEET DOUGH
(page 194)

7OZ (200G) MARZIPAN OR HAZELNUT PASTE
(page 189-190 or ready-made)

1 TEASPOON RUM

1 TEASPOON WHOLE MILK

7OZ (200G) RAISINS, ABOUT 1¼ CUPS RAISINS

½ CUP (150G) APRICOT JAM (optional)
FOR GLAZING

1½ CUPS (150G) CONFECTIONER' SUGAR
(OPTIONAL), FOR ICING

Line two baking sheets with parchment paper or silicone sheets. Prepare the dough as directed on page 194 and leave it to proof at room temperature for about 1 hour. Check it is ready using the poke test (see page 201).

Soften the marzipan by kneading, then cut it into small pieces. Put it in a bowl, add the rum and milk, and mix with your hands until you have a spreadable paste. You might need a bit more milk.

Once the dough is ready, roll it into a rectangle at least 14in (35cm) long, measured from the edge farthest away to the nearest edge. Spread the marzipan mixture over the dough rectangle, leaving a strip of dough about 1in (2cm) uncovered at the short end farthest from you. Sprinkle the raisins over the marzipan. Lightly press the raisins into the dough using a rolling pin or your hands. Roll up the rectangle, starting at the short end nearest you. Once you reach the other end, pinch the seam slightly to seal the roll.

Cut the roll into slices ¾–1in (2–3cm) thick and transfer them onto the lined baking sheets, spaced well apart. Cover and leave the swirls to rise for at least 1 hour, as they need to be well expanded.

Preheat the oven to 375°F (190°C). Bake for about 15 minutes, until they are a rich, golden color. If glazing with apricot jam, heat the jam with a little bit of water and brush it onto the swirls as soon as they are out of the oven.

If you are using a water icing, make this to your liking by adding water to confectioners' sugar, a drop at a time, and apply once the swirls are cool. These are best eaten fresh.

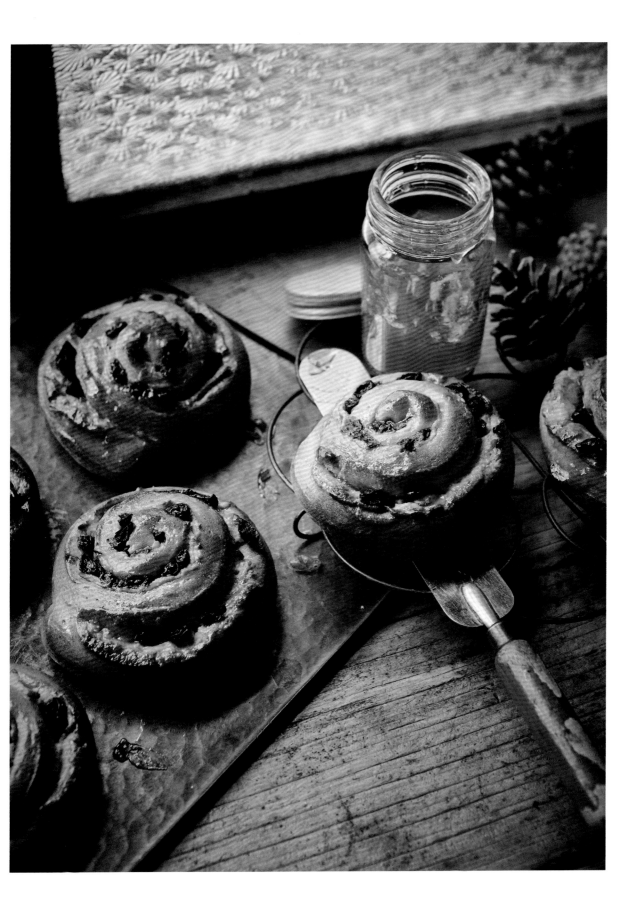

Quark-Streusel Buns
Quark and Crumble Buns

While I was studying physics, these buns were my go-to snacks. In Freiburg, they were on offer in every little bakery outlet, and I would get one and eat it out of a paper bag while strolling through town. The three layers—sweet bread, quark, and streusel—combine beautifully to something simple but delicious, with their differences in flavor and textures.

makes 10

1 PORTION STREUSEL (page 192)

1 PORTION BASIC YEASTED SWEET DOUGH
(page 194)

ALL-PURPOSE FLOUR FOR DUSTING

300G LOW FAT QUARK

⅓ CUP (75G) SUPERFINE SUGAR

2 MEDIUM EGG YOLK

1 TEASPOON VANILLA BEAN PASTE

CONFECTIONERS' SUGAR, FOR SPRINKLING
OR ICING (optional), AS NEEDED

Line two baking sheets with parchment paper or silicone sheets. Prepare the streusel as directed on page 192 and set aside to cool in the fridge. Prepare the dough as directed on page 194 and leave to proof at room temperature for about 1 hour. Check it is ready using the poke test (see page 201).

Once the dough is ready, divide it into 3oz (85g) pieces and shape them to rounds. Place the rounds on a floured surface and cover with a dish towel or a plastic bag and leave to proof at room temperature for 30–45 minutes.

Flatten the rounds into ovals about ½in (1cm) thick, using a rolling pin. Transfer to the baking sheets, cover, and leave to proof again for about 30 minutes. Preheat the oven to 375°F (190°C).

Prepare the filling. Put the quark, sugar, egg yolks, and vanilla bean paste in a bowl and whisk until the sugar has dissolved.

Once the ovals have proofed, make an indentation in the middle using your fist or the back of a ladle. Fill the indentation with quark filling (about 2 tablespoons per bun); there should be a bit of a border of dough visible (about ¼in [5mm]) so that the filling doesn't spill out during baking. Sprinkle the streusel over the filling so that it is mostly covered.

Bake the buns for about 18 minutes, until the streusel starts to color. Transfer to a wire rack to cool. If you want them extra sweet, sprinkle with confectioners' sugar or brush with a stiff icing. To make a stiff icing, sift confectioners' sugar and add water drop by drop while stirring until the icing reaches the desired consistency. These buns are best eaten on the day of baking, but they keep for a couple of days stored in an airtight container.

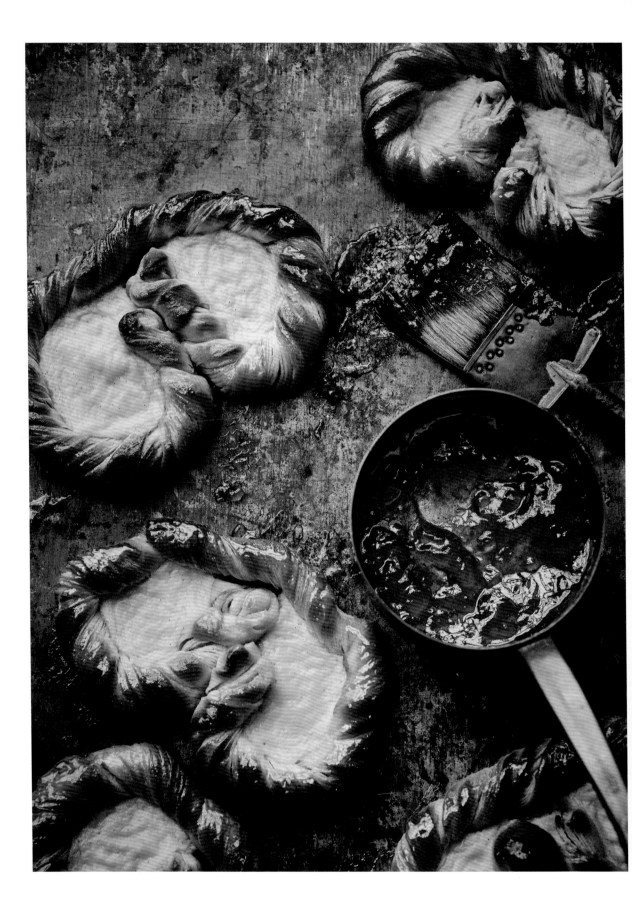

Pudding-Plunder
Custard Danish

There are many things that can be done with Plunder (Danish pastry) dough, but to my mother and me, one of the tastiest is this recipe, which is sometimes also called Pudding-Brezel or Kopenhagener. A long strand of Plunder dough encircles two big "eyes" of vanilla pudding.

Prepare the Plunder dough as directed on page 197. Prepare the vanilla pudding as directed on page 185. Line two baking sheets with parchment paper.

Once the Plunder dough is ready, roll it out to a rectangle about 20in (50cm) long, and ⅛in (3mm) thick. This might be easier if you divide the dough into two portions. Cut the rectangle lengthwise into strips about ¾in (1.5cm) wide. Take one strip and twist it. Shape the twisted strip into a goggles shape. Transfer the shape onto a lined baking sheet. You will be able to place 4–6 Pudding-Plunders on one baking sheet.

Fill the pastry shape with vanilla pudding. Cover the Plunders and leave them to proof for 30 to 60 minutes, depending on room temperature, until they are well puffed up and fragile.

Meanwhile, preheat the oven to 375°F (190°C).

Bake for about 15 minutes, until the pastry is dark golden and the puddings start to catch.

Put the apricot jam, if using, in a saucepan with a splash of water and bring to a boil. Then quickly brush the hot pastries, but not the pudding, with jam.

Leave to cool completely before removing from the parchment paper, otherwise the vanilla pudding will run. These are best eaten fresh, but they will keep for a day in an airtight container.

makes 8–16, depending on size

1 PORTION PLUNDER DOUGH
(page 197)

1 PORTION VANILLA PUDDING WITH EGG
(page 185)

⅓ CUP (100G) APRICOT JAM (optional)

Apfel-Plunder
Apple Turnover

This treat is very easy to make and can serve as a starting point for many experiments. But it is delicious just as it is.

makes 8–12

1 PORTION PLUNDER DOUGH
(page 197)

5 APPLES

3½OZ (100G) RAISINS,
ABOUT A HEAPING ½ CUP RAISINS

2 TABLESPOONS CINNAMON SUGAR
(page 181)

⅓ CUP (100G) APRICOT JAM

Prepare the Plunder dough as directed on page 197.

Peel, core, and finely cube the apples. Mix the apple cubes, raisins, and cinnamon sugar in a bowl and leave to marinate for 30 minutes.

Line two baking sheets with parchment paper.

Once the Plunder dough is ready, roll it out to a rectangle about 16in (40cm) long and ⅛in (3mm) thick. This might be easier if you divide the dough into two portions.

Cut the rectangle into 4in (10cm) squares. Place about 1 tablespoon of apple filling in the center of each square. Fold two opposing corners of the square over the apple filling.

Transfer the Plunders onto the lined baking sheets. Cover and leave to proof for 1–1½ hours, until puffy and fragile.

Meanwhile, preheat the oven to 375°F (190°C).

Bake for about 15 minutes, until the pastry is dark golden.

Put the apricot jam in a saucepan with a splash of water and bring to a boil. Then quickly brush the hot pastries with jam. These are best eaten fresh, but will keep for a day in an airtight container.

Zwiebelkuchen
Onion Tart

Variations of this savory tart can be found in various areas of Germany; in the southwest of Germany, it is a village fair staple. In the Black Forest, it is usually topped with the famous, finely chopped, smoked and cured bacon, but smoked bacon cubes will do, and for a vegetarian version, it is no problem to avoid the bacon completely, bringing the sweet flavors of the onions to the fore.

For the dough, put the flour, yeast, salt, sugar, and milk into a bowl and mix together. If using a stand mixer, knead the dough until a smooth ball forms. If kneading by hand, turn the contents of your bowl out onto a work surface and knead until the dough starts to become smooth and shows some gluten development. Full gluten development is not necessary—a cakelike texture is welcome. Add the butter and knead it in. Cover the dough and leave it to proof at room temperature for at least 1 hour until puffy and well risen.

Preheat the oven to 425°F (220°C). Grease a 9in (23cm) springform cake pan with butter. Roll out the dough into a disk slightly bigger than the pan. Line the pan with the dough—there should be a ½in (1cm) rim all the way around. Cover and set aside.

In a big frying pan, heat the butter and add the onions. Sauté the onions for about 5 minutes on low to medium heat until they have become translucent. Sprinkle the onions with the flour and continue frying for a minute while stirring. Transfer the onions onto a flat dish and leave to cool.

Once the onions have cooled (lukewarm is okay), whisk the heavy cream and eggs together. Transfer the onions to a bowl and add the egg and cream mixture. Season with salt, pepper, and nutmeg.

Once the yeasted base is ready—it should have risen a bit and feel tender to the touch—add the filling and spread evenly. Try to keep the rim of the dough uncovered, so that the filling won't spill over. Sprinkle the caraway seeds and bacon over the top (if using).

Bake for about 45 minutes, until the crust becomes a medium to dark golden-brown. Zwiebelkuchen can be eaten warm, and it goes very well with a hearty drink.

serves 12

FOR THE DOUGH
2 CUPS (250G) BREAD FLOUR

2¼ TEASPOONS INSTANT YEAST

1 TEASPOON SALT

1 TEASPOON SUPERFINE SUGAR

⅔ CUP (150ML) WHOLE MILK, LUKEWARM

3½ UNSALTED BUTTER, SOFTENED,
ROOM TEMPERATURE,
PLUS EXTRA FOR GREASING

FOR THE TOPPING
3½ TABLESPOONS UNSALTED BUTTER

18OZ (500G) WHITE ONIONS, CHOPPED

1 TABLESPOON BREAD FLOUR

½ CUP (100ML) HEAVY CREAM

2 MEDIUM EGGS

SALT, PEPPER, AND NUTMEG TO TASTE

1 TABLESPOON CARAWAY SEEDS

3OZ (75G) BACON CUBES (optional)

Kirsch-Plotzer
Cherry Bread Pudding

I haven't found a translation for the word plotzer—it describes a variety of baked goods that are like bread-and-butter pudding— but with added fruit. The most widespread variety is kirsch-plotzer, which is made with cherries and often uses leftover bread. We had a couple of cherry trees in our garden, and during harvesttime, my mother would sometimes have a plotzer ready as an after-school meal.

In Germany, this pudding is generally made with whole cherries, including the pits! That way it doesn't get too soggy. But it works well without the cherry pits, too. It is usually served with cinnamon sugar, custard, or ice cream.

serves 8–12

10OZ (300G) MILK ROLLS (PAGE 98) OR BAGUETTE

1¾ CUPS (400ML) WHOLE MILK

2–3LB (1–1.5KG) CHERRIES (fresh or from a jar)

3 MEDIUM EGGS, SEPARATED

⅓ CUP (80G) SUPERFINE SUGAR

7 TABLESPOONS (100G) UNSALTED BUTTER, CUBED, ROOM TEMPERATURE, PLUS EXTRA FOR GREASING

2 TABLESPOONS KIRSCH OR BRANDY

2 TABLESPOONS GROUND CINNAMON

¼ TEASPOON GROUND CLOVES

½ TEASPOON GROUND NUTMEG

1¾ CUPS (180G) HAZELNUTS, GROUND

Cut the bread into thin slices. Bring the milk to a boil, then remove from the heat. Soak the bread in the hot milk and leave to cool.

Preheat the oven to 350°F (180°C). Grease a 10in (25cm) springform cake pan, or a similar deep oven dish.

If you are using cherries from a jar, drain them well. If using fresh cherries, wash them and remove the stems. Remove the cherry pits, if desired.

Beat the egg whites to soft peaks.

Mix the sugar, butter, egg yolks, kirsch, cinnamon, cloves, nutmeg, and hazelnuts with the bread and milk mixture. If this is very stiff, add a little more milk. Fold in the egg whites. Finally, fold in the cherries.

Transfer the dough to your prepared pan and bake for 1 hour to 1 hour 20 minutes, or until the top is crisp but not too dark.

If using a springform pan, let it cool a bit before taking out of the pan.

Kirsch-Plotzer is best eaten warm, but it keeps for a few days in an airtight container and tastes nice cold as well.

WITH MY BROTHER CELEBRATING CHRISTMAS AT MY GRANDPARENTS' PLACE.
THE TABLE HELD AN INTRICATE LANDSCAPE MADE WITH FRESHLY COLLECTED
MOSS AND THE THREE KINGS APPROACHING THE STABLE.

Festive bakes

*I*n this chapter, I present some seasonal recipes, baked goods, and traditions that we cherished in our family. The big occasion for baking in Germany is, of course, Christmas. Many of the German cookies and cakes store very well and, in fact, improve over time. So, the four weeks of Advent, which is the time for spiritual preparation for Christmas, is also a time to bake for the festival.

We started baking in our family around the 1st of December. Every Saturday leading up to Christmas, my mother, brother, and I would bake several batches of cookies, which then got added to a huge cake pan. My mother gave us almost free choice of what to make, and we had great joy in looking through cookbooks to find a recipe we would like to bake. Of course, there were lots of mishaps, but they were all tasty. In the end, we would have around 12 different kinds of cookies in that big pan. This chapter includes some of my all-time favorites.

Our family started the New Year by having a giant decorated sweet pretzel for breakfast, and buttered slices were also offered to visitors who came to wish us good luck, as was the custom in our area. The pretzels were made from a simple enriched dough, sometimes with a hint of cardamom and lemon, and they were highly decorated with braids, lucky symbols, sheafs of wheat, and the numbers of the new year starting. Initially, we ordered them at a local bakery, but as we all grew more confident, we started making our own, and it was huge fun creating all those decorations.

Carnival was a very special time. Marking the last days before Lent, people liked to go crazy and dress up. On Maundy Thursday, an evening parade marked the beginning of the feast. Everybody wore pyjamas or nighties, and the brass band led the procession through the village to the town square, where a symbolic transfer of power from the mayor to the fool's guild took place. I am sure I had my first sip of glühwein on one of those occasions. On Saturday, there was the evening event for adults, and on Sunday afternoon, the children's party with dressing up, fun games, lots of food, and a brass band (I went once as a female spy from *The Avengers*—wearing my mother's clothes, my aunt's swim cap, and with a toy gun in my handbag). On Monday and Tuesday, the streets of Freiburg were full of people in costume, with members of the organized fool's guilds in their weird and wondrous costumes.

To provide the energy for all that fooling around, the bakeries were full of deep-fried pastries, such as crullers, doughnuts, and the more regional specialties included in this book. My grandma was always the first to treat us to a bag of Scherben, a wafer-thin, crisp pastry.

At Easter, all the sweets held back during Lent were suddenly abundant: the stores were full of chocolate eggs and candy bunnies and treats for the egg hunt. As a tonic to all this sweetness, most families would bring out a braided Easter loaf, which is not too sweet and is filled with raisins and topped with almonds. The recipe I have included is one that we like in our family.

serves about 10

¼ CUP (60G) UNSALTED BUTTER

9OZ (250ML) WHOLE MILK, COLD

4 CUPS (500G) BREAD FLOUR

¼ CUP (60G) SUPERFINE SUGAR

½ TEASPOON SALT

2¼ TEASPOONS INSTANT YEAST

1 MEDIUM EGG

½ TEASPOON GROUND CARDAMOM

ZEST OF 1 LEMON

1 MEDIUM EGG, BEATEN,
FOR GLAZING

Neujahrs-Brezel
New Year Pretzel

Bakeries can make huge custom brezeln in their deck ovens, which can be 1 yard or more in diameter and very elaborately decorated. A brezel made of 1¾lb (800g) of dough just about fits into a standard domestic oven. This recipe makes about nearly 2lb (900g), so you have 3½oz (100g) of dough to go wild on your decorations!

Melt the butter in a saucepan. Once melted, add the milk and take off the heat. This will give the milk just the right temperature.

Put all the ingredients, except the egg for the glaze, in a big bowl. Mix with your hands or a stand mixer fitted with the dough hook. Once all the ingredients are well incorporated, knead the dough until a smooth ball forms and the gluten is developed. Cover and leave to proof for about 1½ hours at room temperature.

Once well risen, divide the dough into 2 balls—one weighing 28oz, or 1¾lb (800g) and the other 3½oz (100g). Set the small amount of dough aside, covered, in a cool place. This is for the decoration.

For shaping the pretzel, you need a lot of space. Shape the large dough ball into a log. While shaping, it is very important that you don't tear the dough. For instructions on how to shape logs, see page 201. If the dough feels like it is fighting you, give it a couple of minutes' rest to relax the gluten and then continue working on it—rolling it gently until you have a long, even strand of dough, aim for 7ft (220cm) length. Line a large baking sheet with a silicone sheet or parchment paper (stuck down with a bit of butter) and place the dough so that the midpoint of the strand lies in the center of the baking sheet but close to the edge farthest

away from you. Continue shaping the pretzel as illustrated on the pages 103 and 104. Press the ends of the strands slightly so that they bond with the body of the pretzel. Cover the pretzel with a dish towel and set aside, ideally in a cool place.

Take the remaining dough and create the decorations. To decorate, you can use small amounts of dough and braid them. Make the numbers of the year by rolling pieces of dough into a thread, or use cookie cutters. Popular decorations are also little pig shapes, ladders, and toadstools, things that in Germany are associated with good luck. Stick the decorations to the pretzel with a bit of the beaten egg.

Once all decorations are applied, leave the pretzel to rise for another 30 minutes or so, depending on how long it took to decorate. All in all, from dividing the dough to putting the pretzel in the oven should take about 1½–2 hours.

Preheat the oven to 350°F (180°C).

Once the pretzel is ready, brush it with beaten egg and bake it for about 25 minutes. The color should be light golden.

This is best eaten fresh, but it keeps in an airtight container for a few days and is also nice toasted. Shown on pages 136–137.

Mutzenmandeln

These are made of an almond-rich pastry, deep-fried and doused in cinnamon sugar. They are roughly shaped like an almond. They can be kept for a few days.

*makes 30–50,
depending on the size of cutter*

3 MEDIUM EGGS

⅔ CUP (125G) SUPERFINE SUGAR

⅓ CUP (85G) UNSALTED BUTTER,
ROOM TEMPERATURE

⅔ CUP (60G) GROUND ALMONDS

2¾ CUPS (370G) ALL-PURPOSE FLOUR,
PLUS EXTRA FOR DUSTING

1 TEASPOON RUM

1 TEASPOON BAKING POWDER

1 PINCH SALT

VEGETABLE OIL FOR FRYING

CINNAMON SUGAR, AS NEEDED
(page 181)

Put all the ingredients, except for the oil and cinnamon sugar, in a bowl and mix well using your hands. The resulting dough will be quite soft and a bit sticky. Roll out the dough on a well-floured surface to about ⅓in (8mm) thick.

Use a heart-shaped cookie cutter (about 1½in [4cm] wide) to cut out hearts. Cut the hearts in half to get almond-shaped pieces of dough.

Add enough oil for deep-frying to a deep, heavy saucepan or deep-fat fryer, making sure it is no more than two-thirds full and heat to 350°F (180°C). A wooden spoon dipped into the oil should release lots of bubbles. Try with a small piece of dough first—it should fry quickly, with loads of bubbles.

Deep-fry the Mutzenmandeln in batches for 3 minutes on each side until they are a deep golden-brown.

When ready, transfer them onto a piece of paper towel to drain the surplus oil. While still warm, douse them in cinnamon sugar. These are best eaten fresh, but will keep for 3 to 4 days.

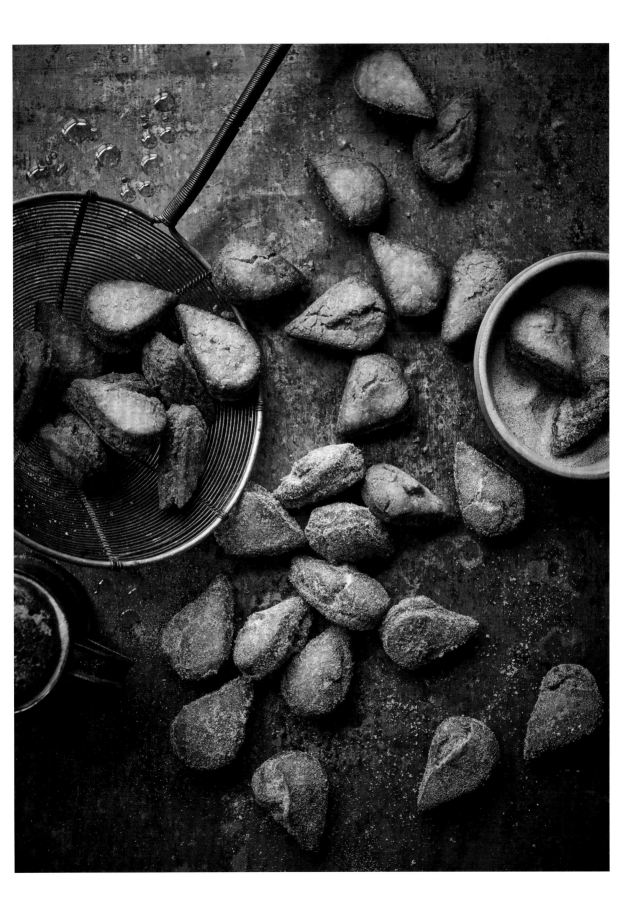

Scherben
Shards

With their highly irregular twisted shapes, their surface covered in bubbles and their crispy texture, these deep-fried pastries are just as exciting to look at as they are to bite into. They derive their name from pieces of broken pottery.

serves 6

1 MEDIUM EGG YOLK

2 MEDIUM EGGS

3½ TABLESPOONS UNSALTED BUTTER, AT ROOM TEMPERATURE

2 TABLESPOONS RUM

5 TABLESPOONS (70ML) MADEIRA WINE

3¼ CUPS (400G) ALL-PURPOSE FLOUR, PLUS EXTRA FOR DUSTING

VEGETABLE OIL FOR DEEP-FRYING

CONFECTIONERS' SUGAR FOR DUSTING

Put all the ingredients, except for the oil and confectioners' sugar, in a bowl. Mix with your hands or in a stand mixer fitted with the dough hook until the dough forms a smooth ball. Flatten the dough, wrap in plastic wrap and let it rest for 30 minutes.

Add enough oil for deep-frying to a deep, heavy saucepan or deep-fat fryer, making sure it is no more than two-thirds full and heat to 350°F (180°C). A wooden spoon dipped into the oil should release lots of bubbles. Line a baking sheet or big plate with paper towels.

Cut the dough into six pieces. On a lightly floured surface, roll out each piece very thinly (paper thin, less than 1mm thick). Cut each one into diamonds about 3½in (8cm) long. The shapes don't matter too much, as this pastry is always quite irregular.

Deep-fry no more than two pieces at a time for about 3 minutes, until they are light golden-brown at the center, with darker edges. Take the shards out of the oil and transfer them to the lined sheet or plate to remove surplus oil. Dust with confectioners' sugar while still warm. Repeat until the dough is used up.

These shards are best enjoyed fresh, but they will keep for 2 days in a sealed food bag or an airtight container.

Oster-Zopf mit Yoghurt
Easter Braid with Yogurt

A braided, sweet bread is great food to share on Easter Sunday morning, when family and neighbors visit, and children are preparing to go on their egg hunt. A slice of this braid, smothered with butter, and a cup of coffee, is a simple and great way to start this holiday. But this Easter braid tastes just as good on any other occasion all year round.

Preheat the oven to 350°F (180C). Line a baking sheet with a silicone sheet or parchment paper.

Sift both flours, the baking powder, salt, vanilla sugar, and superfine sugar into a bowl. Add the yogurt, milk, oil, lemon zest, and whole eggs and mix, either by hand or with a stand mixer fitted with the dough hook. Once the ingredients are well distributed, knead the dough until it starts showing some gluten development. Add the raisins and work them into the dough. Don't overwork the dough. This dough feels extremely fragile and soft, therefore, work quickly, and use plenty of flour to avoid stickiness.

Divide the dough into three equal portions. Shape each portion into a long sausage and transfer them to the baking sheet, placing the sausages next to each other. Braid the sausages and pinch the ends of the braid together.

Beat the egg yolk and milk together to make the egg wash. Brush the braid with egg wash and sprinkle liberally with flaked almonds.

Bake the braid for about 50 minutes, until the braid and almonds have a nice golden color. Leave to cool. This Easter braid keeps very well, and after a few days still tastes great when toasted. Store in an airtight container for up to 5 days.

serves 20

2 CUPS (250G) BREAD FLOUR

2 CUPS (250G) ALL-PURPOSE FLOUR

3½ TEASPOONS BAKING POWDER

1 PINCH SALT

2 TEASPOONS STRONG VANILLA SUGAR
(page 180)

⅓ CUP (80G) SUPERFINE SUGAR

9OZ (250G) YOGURT

¼ CUP (50ML) WHOLE MILK

⅓ CUP (80ML) VEGETABLE OIL

ZEST OF 1 LEMON

2 MEDIUM EGGS

5OZ (140G) RAISINS, A HEAPING ¾ CUP RAISINS

1 MEDIUM EGG YOLK, FOR EGG WASH

1 TABLESPOON WHOLE MILK
FOR EGG WASH

FLAKED ALMONDS, AS NEEDED

Spritz-Ringe
Crullers

Interestingly, we rarely had this pastry at home, but I have strong memories of seeing them in bakeries around Carnival time when I was little. Here is the recipe to fulfill my longings from back then.

makes 10

1¾ CUPS (225G) BREAD FLOUR

⅔ CUP (185ML) WHOLE MILK

¾ CUP (180G) UNSALTED BUTTER,
ROOM TEMPERATURE

2 TABLESPOONS SUPERFINE SUGAR

½ TEASPOON SALT

6 EGGS

VEGETABLE OIL FOR DEEP-FRYING

1 CUP (100G) CONFECTIONERS' SUGAR, SIFTED

WATER, AS NEEDED

To make the choux pastry (or *brand-teig*, in German), draw 10 circles the size of your rings (about the diameter of a mug) with a pencil onto parchment paper. Cut the paper into 10 squares so that each square contains one ring. Set aside. Sift the flour into a bowl and set aside.

Put the milk, butter, sugar, and salt into a saucepan. Very gently heat until the butter is melted, then bring to a rolling boil. Take off the heat and, with a wooden spoon, beat the flour into the milk until all flour is incorporated. Put back onto the heat and keep beating—the dough is cooked enough when the bottom of the saucepan is covered in a white, thin crust. Transfer the dough to a big bowl and continue beating until the dough is lukewarm.

Break the eggs into a bowl and beat them lightly. Add a bit of beaten egg to the dough and beat until the egg is fully absorbed. Repeat until the dough has the right consistency: it should be shiny and drop off the spoon in sheets, and it should hold its shape well.

In a deep-fat fryer or deep, heavy saucepan, heat the oil to 365°F (185°C), making sure the pan is no more than two-thirds full.

Transfer the choux dough into a piping bag with a big French star nozzle. With the pencil side facing down, pipe one ring onto your template. Pipe an identical ring on top of the first ring. Pipe two of these double rings, and then drop them immediately into the oil. Deep-fry on one side until golden (about 1½ minutes). Take the papers out of the oil as soon as they become loose—chopsticks are great for this. Turn the rings over and fry the other side. Once done, transfer them to a plate lined with paper towels to drain some of the oil. Repeat this process until you have used all of the dough.

Once the rings are cool, make a slightly runny water icing; sift the confectioners' sugar, then stir in water a drop at a time, until the desired consistency is reached. Glaze the rings. Eat within a few hours.

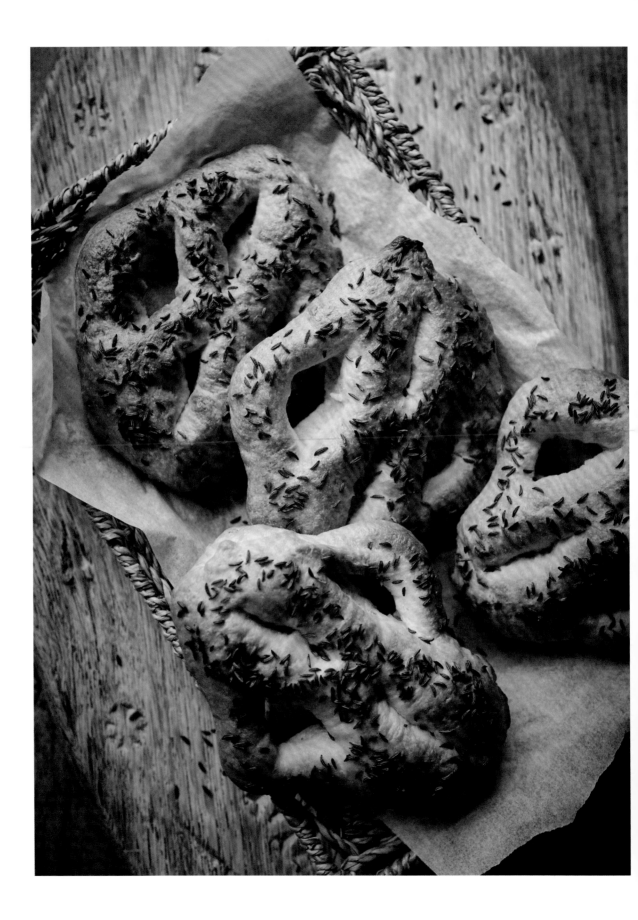

Fastenwähe

This attractive roll is a Lent specialty from Basel in Switzerland. During Lent, you can buy it on every street corner. The tradition of this roll goes back hundreds of years; there is an iron tool from the fifteenth century for creating the characteristic shape. I came across them when I was in Basel with my musical friends and I fell in love with them. That is why, after starting to make bread, I tried to make them here in England, and this recipe is the result. The original recipes use lard, but butter or goose fat work as well. Goose fat retains the crust and texture that lard creates. With butter, it will be more like a brioche.

If using butter, melt the butter in a microwave or in a bowl in hot water. Line two baking sheets with parchment paper or silicone sheet.

Put the flour, salt, honey, yeast, and milk in a bowl and mix using your hands, or a stand mixer fitted with the dough hook. Once gluten starts to form and all ingredients are well integrated, add the fat. Incorporate the fat and knead until the dough forms a smooth ball and the gluten is well developed. Cover and leave to proof at room temperature for about 1 hour.

Check that the dough is ready using the poke test (see page 201), then divide it into eight equal pieces (about 3½oz [100g]). Shape them into logs or batons about 4in (10cm) long. Place four logs well spaced on each baking sheet. Cover with a dish towel and leave to prove at room temperature for about 1 hour. When ready, they should be puffy, but not too fragile. They shouldn't deflate when cutting them.

Preheat the oven to 425°F (220°C).

Once the rolls have proofed, take a spatula about 1½in (4cm) long with a straight edge or a knife. Make two slits into each roll, right down the middle, so that there is a bit of dough between the two slits, like this: - - Then make two more slits, parallel to the middle ones, so there is one slit on either side of the midline. Pull the sides of the rolls, where you made the last two slits, until you get a shape that is very roughly circular, with four holes in it (see photo). Spray or brush the rolls with water and liberally top with caraway seeds.

Bake for about 15 minutes, until rich golden-brown. They are delicious just as they are. They are best eaten fresh, but will keep for a day in an airtight container.

makes 6

⅔ CUP (150G) FAT
(lard, goose fat, unsalted butter)

3½ CUPS (400G) BREAD FLOUR

1 HEAPING TEASPOON SALT

1 TEASPOON HONEY

2½ TEASPOONS INSTANT YEAST

9OZ (250ML) WHOLE MILK, LUKEWARM

WATER FOR GLAZING

CARAWAY SEEDS FOR SPRINKLING

Spiegelei
Fried Egg

Beacause Easter has such a strong connection to eggs, bakers created a "fried egg" pastry for the occasion, a yeasted bun dusted in confectioners' sugar, with an "egg yolk" apricot sitting in some custard. Simple as it is, the look and the different textures always make this a seasonal favorite!

makes about 12 buns

1 PORTION BASIC YEASTED SWEET DOUGH
(page 194)

½ PORTION VANILLA PUDDING WITH EGG
(page 185)

ALL-PURPOSE FLOUR FOR DUSTING

14½OZ (410G) CAN APRICOT HALVES
IN SYRUP, DRAINED

CONFECTIONERS' SUGAR FOR DUSTING

Make the dough as directed on page 194.

Make the pudding as directed on page 185.

After the first proof, divide the dough into 3oz (80g) pieces. Shape those pieces into balls and transfer them to floured baking sheets. Leave some space between them so they don't touch each other. Cover and leave to proof at room temperature for about 30 minutes.

On a floured surface, using a rolling pin, roll the balls into flat, oval shapes about 1in (2cm) thick, and transfer them back to the baking sheet. Cover and leave to proof for another 30 minutes.

Preheat the oven to 375°F (190°C).

Sprinkle a bit of flour near one focal point on an oval—where you want to put your yolk—and make a depression with a ladle. Fill the depression with 1 tablespoon of pudding. Place an apricot half, cut-side down, on the pudding and squeeze gently. Repeat with the remaining ovals and filling.

Bake for about 12 minutes, until the buns are medium golden. Transfer the buns to a wire rack and dust with confectioners' sugar. These are best eaten on the same day as baking.

Bethmännchen

These are very easy to make and able to withstand a long shaping session by children. In fact, these might have been some of the first cookies I ever made. Being a specialty from Frankfurt, they are available there all year round. In the rest of Germany, they are more of a Christmas treat. Bethmännchen work perfectly well made with gluten-free flour.

makes about 40

3½OZ (100G) BLANCHED ALMONDS

7OZ (200G) MARZIPAN
(page 189 or ready-made)

1 CUP (100G) GROUND ALMONDS

¾ CUP (75G) CONFECTIONERS' SUGAR, SIFTED

⅓ CUP (40G) ALL-PURPOSE FLOUR
(or gluten-free flour)

1 MEDIUM EGG

1 TEASPOON ALMOND EXTRACT

1 MEDIUM EGG YOLK FOR GLAZING

Split the whole almonds in half and reserve for decoration.

Line a baking tray with parchment paper.

Cut the marzipan into pieces and put it into a bowl. Add the ground almonds, confectioners' sugar, flour, egg, and almond extract and knead by hand until a smooth ball forms. Cover in plastic wrap and let it rest in the fridge for about 30 minutes.

Preheat the oven to 350°F (180°C).

Once rested, shape the dough into little balls the size of a big cherry or a small walnut. You can do this by dividing the dough, then rolling it to two strands to the diameter you want and cutting those strands into appropriately sized chunks. Roll these chunks into spheres between your palms.

Decorate each ball with three almond halves, the tips of the almonds pointing into the center. Put the decorated Bethmännchen onto the prepared baking sheet. Once the sheet is full, glaze with egg yolk.

Bake for about 20 minutes—the tops should be golden, while they should still be very light near the bottom. They keep in an airtight container for several weeks.

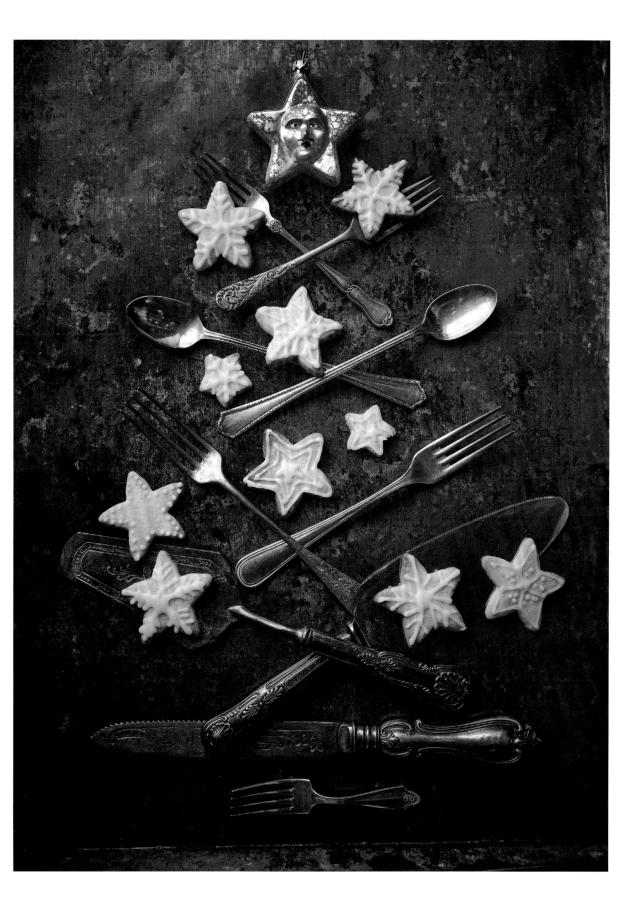

Butter-Kekse
Butter Cookies

*makes about 60,
depending on
size of the cutter*

3¾ CUPS (380G) ALL-PURPOSE FLOUR,
PLUS EXTRA FOR DUSTING

5½ TABLESPOONS (50G) CORNSTARCH

1 TEASPOON BAKING POWDER

1 PINCH SALT

1¾ CUPS (200G) CONFECTIONERS' SUGAR

2 TEASPOONS VANILLA SUGAR (PAGE 181)
OR VANILLA BEAN PASTE

ZEST OF 1 LEMON

1 MEDIUM EGG

1 CUP + 2 TABLESPOONS (250G)
UNSALTED BUTTER, SOFTENED, CUBED

2 TABLESPOONS WHOLE MILK

1 MEDIUM EGG YOLK (optional) FOR GLAZING

LEMON JUICE (optional) FOR LEMON ICING

CONFECTIONERS' SUGAR (optional)
FOR LEMON ICING

SPRINKLES (optional)

FOOD COLORING (optional)

As children, these were our all-time Christmas favorites and decorating them got me so excited that sometimes the finished article was more decoration than cookie. The dough is quite soft, which means that children's hands will find it easy to mix. From my experience, the dough is also quite resilient against overworking. Like most German Christmas cookies, these will be better after a while, stored in an airtight container.

Sift the flour, cornstarch, baking powder, and salt together into a bowl. Add the remaining ingredients except for the optional finishes and mix with your hands or in a stand mixer fitted with the dough hook, until a smooth dough forms. This dough will be very soft. Remove the dough from the bowl, wrap it in plastic wrap and put it in the fridge for at least 1 hour.

Once the dough is cool and firm, preheat the oven to 350°F (180°C). Line two baking sheets with parchment paper.

Roll out portions of the dough on a floured surface, about ⅛in (3mm) thick. Using cookie cutters of your choice, stamp out the cookies and transfer them to the prepared baking sheets. Apply egg yolk for glazing, if desired.

Bake the cookies for 10 minutes, until the edges start to brown a bit. Leave to cool for a minute before transferring the cookies to a wire rack to cool completely. Decorate the cookies if you like—there are no limits. Classics are lemon glaze (mix sifted confectioners' sugar with a few drops of lemon juice to get a smooth spreadable consistency) plus sprinkles, and egg yolk and sprinkles (applied before baking).

Shown on pages 152–153.

Marzipan-Spritzgebäck
Marzipan Swirls

Because my brother and I liked marzipan a lot, these cookies, which are a bit like Viennese swirls, caught our eye, and they had the benefit of using an exciting tool: a pastry syringe.

makes about 50

2 MEDIUM EGGS

7OZ (200G) MARZIPAN
(page 189 or ready-made)

⅓ CUP (70G) SUPERFINE SUGAR

½ TEASPOON ALMOND EXTRACT

7OZ (200G) UNSALTED BUTTER, CUBED

1¾ CUPS (200G) ALL-PURPOSE FLOUR

5½ TABLESPOONS (50G) CORNSTARCH

DARK CHOCOLATE (54% cocoa solids)
(optional), MELTED

COCONUT FLAKES (optional)

Preheat the oven to 375°F (190°C). Line two baking sheets with silicone sheets or parchment paper. Prepare a piping bag with a medium star nozzle.

Separate the eggs. Grate the marzipan, and stir it into the egg whites. Mix until smooth. Avoid incorporating air.

In a separate bowl, mix the sugar, almond extract, and butter until smooth. Incorporate the egg yolks until combined.

Add the marzipan mix, flour, and cornstarch to the butter and sugar and gently mix with your hands to get a smooth paste.

Transfer the dough to the piping bag and pipe shapes of your liking onto the prepared baking sheets—leave enough space between the shapes so that they can spread a bit. Freeze the piped shapes for 10 minutes before baking.

Bake for about 8 minutes; the ridges should just start to brown. Leave the cookies to cool on the baking sheets for a couple of minutes, then transfer them to a wire rack to cool completely.

Once cool, the swirls can be decorated, if desired. Dip the ends of the swirls into melted dark chocolate. You can then sprinkle coconut flakes or sprinkles onto the chocolate, if you wish.

These cookies improve greatly over time when stored in an airtight container.

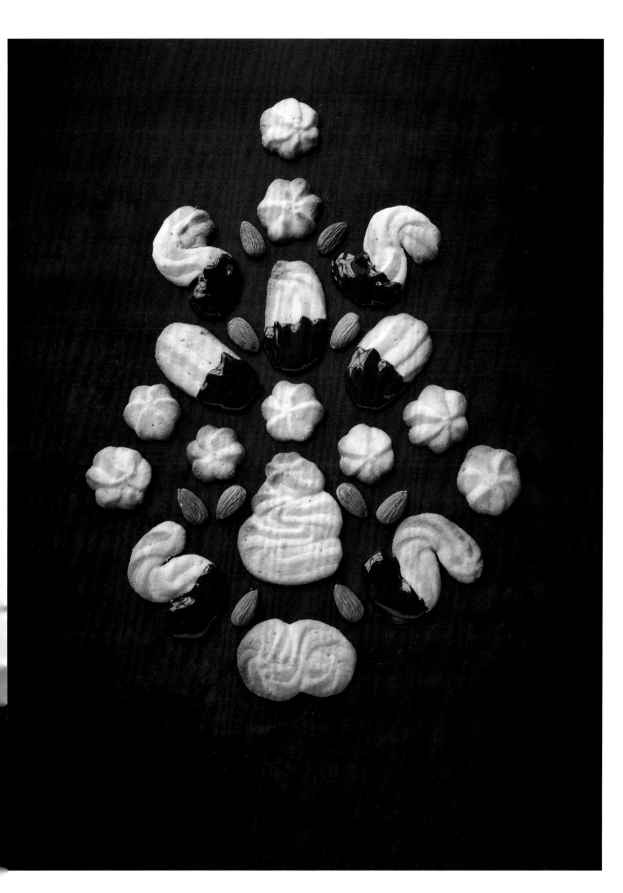

Hilda-Brötle

*These got their name from Hilda von Nassau, Duchess of Baden;
the Black Forest, where I come from, is part of that county.
In other areas they are called by different names—Spitzbuben,
Linzer Augen, etc. Our village baker made them all year round,
about palm size, with three small holes in the top, and often my
grandmother would treat me to one of them. A smaller version is
more specific for Christmas, as given in this recipe.*

*makes 30–50,
depending on
size of cutter*

¼ CUP (50G) SUPERFINE SUGAR

⅔ CUP (150G) UNSALTED BUTTER, CUBED

1 MEDIUM EGG YOLK

1 PINCH SALT

2 TEASPOONS VANILLA SUGAR
(page 180)

2 CUPS (250G) ALL-PURPOSE FLOUR, SIFTED,
PLUS EXTRA FOR DUSTING

CONFECTIONERS' SUGAR FOR DUSTING

¾ CUP (200G) JAM
(raspberry, red currant, or
similar, without seeds)

1 TABLESPOON WATER

Preheat the oven to 350°F (180°C). Line a baking sheet with
parchment paper.

Put the superfine sugar and butter in a bowl and beat until frothy
and light. Beat in the egg yolk, salt, and vanilla sugar. Add the
sifted flour and, with your hands, mix until you have a smooth,
pliable dough.

Roll out the dough on a lightly floured surface until ⅛in (3mm)
thick and cut out cookies with a 2½–3in (6–6cm) diameter fluted
cookie cutter. Transfer the cookies to the prepared baking sheet.
Cut out and remove the centers of half the cookies with a smaller
cutter—a big piping nozzle or the screw cap of a bottle work well.

Bake for about 10 minutes until light golden. Transfer to a wire rack
and leave to cool.

Once cool, place the cookies with a hole precisely on top of the full
cookies. Dust with confectioners' sugar.

Put the jam into a saucepan, add the water, and bring to a boil.
Using a spoon, carefully pour hot jam into the holes in the cookies.
Leave to cool. Store in an airtight container and they will keep for
several weeks.

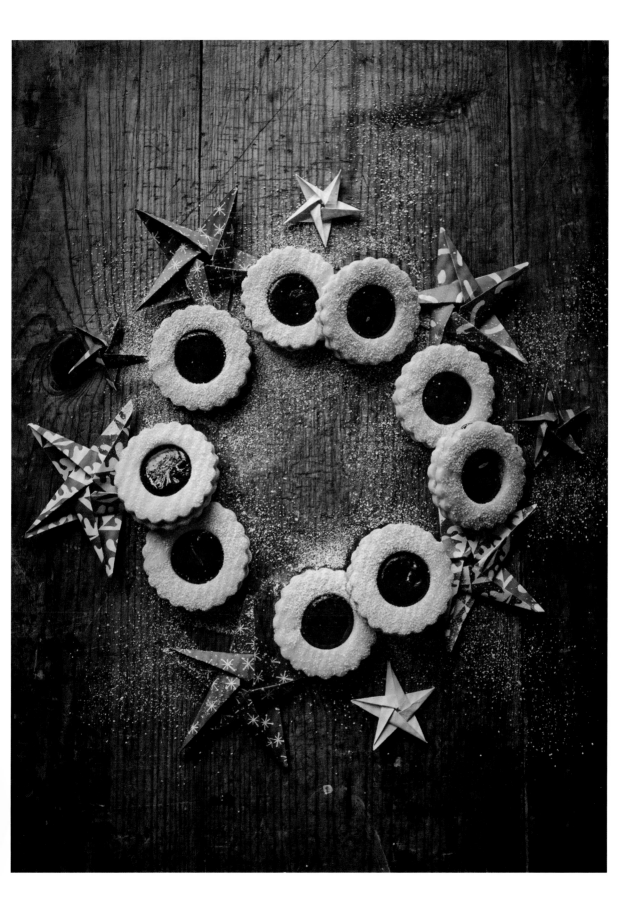

Quark Stollen

This stollen is a great-tasting alternative to the classic Dresdner stollen—it is flavorful, keeps well, and can be eaten right away! And it will get even better over time if you manage to hold yourself back. Greek yogurt or strained cottage cheese can be also used instead of quark. If using cottage cheese, squeeze it through a sieve to get a smooth texture.

serves 20

2 CUPS (250G) BREAD FLOUR

2 CUPS (250G) ALL-PURPOSE FLOUR,
PLUS EXTRA FOR DUSTING

3½ TEASPOONS BAKING POWDER

¾ CUP (150G) SUPERFINE SUGAR

1 CUP (100G) GROUND ALMONDS

2 MEDIUM EGGS

9OZ (250G) QUARK OR GREEK YOGURT

ZEST AND JUICE OF 1 LEMON

1 PINCH SALT

⅔ CUP (150G) UNSALTED BUTTER, CUBED,
ROOM TEMPERATURE

4 TEASPOONs RUM

⅔ CUP (100G) RAISINS

⅔ CUP (100G) CURRANTS

⅔ CUP (100G) MIXED PEEL

7 TABLESPOONS (100G)
UNSALTED BUTTER FOR COATING

1 CUP (100G) CONFECTIONERS' SUGAR, SIFTED,
FOR COATING

Preheat the oven to 350°F (180°C). Line a baking sheet with parchment paper.

Sift both flours and the baking powder into a bowl. Add the sugar and ground almonds and mix. Add the eggs, quark, lemon zest and juice, salt, butter, and rum.

Using your hands or a stand mixer fitted with the dough hook, mix to incorporate all the ingredients, then knead the dough for a few minutes until it becomes smooth and holds together. Work the raisins, currants, and mixed peel into the dough.

On a floured work surface, shape the dough into a rectangle of about 12 x 10in (30 x 25cm). Grab one of the long edges and gently fold it over so that the edge comes up to about 2in (5cm) from the opposite edge to create the typical stollen shape. Transfer the stollen to the prepared baking sheet.

Bake for 1 hour–1 hour, 15 minutes. The color should be a dark golden-brown.

Melt the butter for coating; it should just be just melted, so do not overheat.

Once the stollen is ready and has cooled a bit, liberally douse it in melted butter. Leave to cool completely, then coat with confectioners' sugar. This stollen is ready to eat right away, but it will improve over time if stored in an airtight container. It keeps for about a week.

Printen

Printen are gingerbread-like cookies that were always present at our Christmas celebrations. There are many versions. The Printen cookies we had were rarely homemade—they were one of those seasonal goodies where the commercial quality was just so good that there was no point in making them, at least in our household. For us children, messing around with shaped cookies, a piping syringe was a lot more fun than cutting rectangles, as this recipe demands. However, as I found later, these wonderfully spiced cookies are actually very quick to make.

Preheat the oven to 350°F (180°C). Line a baking sheet with parchment paper.

Sift the flour, sugar, spices, baking powder, and baking ammonia into a bowl. Mix together the honey, coffee, and melted butter, then pour this into the flour mixture. Knead with your hands or a stand mixer fitted with the dough hook until you get a smooth ball. If you like more crunch, add the sugar crystals at this stage; the crystals should be coarse-grained.

Roll out the dough on a lightly floured surface until ¼–½in (6–10mm) thick. Cut the dough into rectangles of about 2½–1in (6–3cm). Transfer the rectangles to the prepared baking sheet. There should be about 1in (3cm) space between the cookies. If you want to decorate with blanched almonds, apply the decoration now.

Bake for about 11 minutes until light brown with darker edges. Leave to cool and glaze as you wish. You can leave the printen unglazed, ice them, or coat them in chocolate. Egg white works well if you used almonds for decoration—apply the egg white thinly when the cookies come out of the oven and are still hot.

As with most German Christmas cookies, these printen will get softer over time and improve hugely when stored in an airtight container. They will keep for at least 6 weeks.

makes about 30

2¾ CUPS (380G) ALL-PURPOSE FLOUR, PLUS EXTRA FOR DUSTING

¾ CUP (150G) SUPERFINE SUGAR

1 TEASPOON GROUND CORIANDER

½ TEASPOON GROUND CLOVES

½ TEASPOON ANISEED, WHOLE

2 TEASPOONS BAKING POWDER

1 TEASPOON BAKING AMMONIA
(or more baking powder)

½ CUP (150G) HONEY

5 TABLESPOONS (75ML) COFFEE, BREWED, VERY STRONG

1 TABLESPOON UNSALTED BUTTER, MELTED

1 TABLESPOON SUGAR CRYSTALS (optional), CRUSHED

BLANCHED ALMONDS (optional) FOR DECORATION

CONFECTIONERS' SUGAR (optional) FOR GLAZE

DARK CHOCOLATE (optional) FOR GLAZE

EGG WHITE (optional) FOR GLAZE

Christmas Stollen, Dresden-Style

serves 20

FOR THE STARTER

2 CUPS (250G) BREAD FLOUR

2¼ TEASPOONS INSTANT YEAST

9OZ (250ML) HEAVY CREAM

FOR THE DOUGH

2 CUPS (250G) RAISINS

2 CUPS (250G) SULTANAS

2 CUPS (250G) CURRANTS

3½OZ (100ML) RUM

½ CUP (100ML) BOILING WATER

2 CUPS (250G) BREAD FLOUR

4 CUPS (500G) ALL-PURPOSE FLOUR

⅔ CUP (125G) SUPERFINE SUGAR

2¼ TEASPOONS INSTANT YEAST

¾ TEASPOON GROUND MACE

¾ TEASPOON GROUND CARDAMOM

¾ TEASPOON GROUND CINNAMON

ZEST OF 2 LEMONS

2¼ CUPS (250G) UNSALTED BUTTER,
CUBED, ROOM TEMPERATURE

1⅓ CUPS (200G) MIXED PEEL

2 CUPS (200G) GROUND ALMONDS

1 CUP + 2 TABLESPOONS (250G)
UNSALTED BUTTER, MELTED, FOR COATING

2¼ CUPS (250G) CONFECTIONERS' SUGAR
FOR COATING

The most famous and celebrated Stollen is Dresdner Stollen, now trademarked, from the city of Dresden in Saxony. It is loaded with fruit and is made with heavy cream and lots of butter. For me, it is inseparable from Christmas. Usually, my parents would be given a Stollen as a Christmas gift and it was a real treat on the coffee table. It keeps extremely well and needs several weeks to mature and unfold all its flavors.

For the starter, mix the flour, instant yeast, and cream together and leave to stand at room temperature for 1 hour. Then place the starter in the fridge overnight.

Place the raisins, golden raisins, and currants in a bowl. Add the rum. Pour as much of the boiling water over the fruit as needed to just cover them. Cover with plastic wrap and leave to stand overnight.

The next day, prepare the dough. Mix together the starter, both flours, sugar, yeast, spices, and lemon zest. Work the butter into this mix and knead. This might seem impossible at first, but it will come together nicely. I like to do this in a 10-quart (liter) bowl using my hands. Normal household mixers won't be able to cope with this dough.

Drain the dried fruit and add to the dough, along with the mixed peel and ground almonds, and incorporate into the dough. Again, this might seem like a hard task, but with a big plastic spatula and a lot of patience it will come together.

Using your hands, push the dough into a rectangle and fold it lengthwise onto itself. Use a bit of flour if it gets too sticky. You can make one large Stollen or a few smaller ones, but I wouldn't recommend making Stollen smaller than 1¾lb (800g); I find larger Stollen give a better texture. Transfer the Stollen onto a lined baking sheet and leave to proof at room temperature for about 2 hours. The Stollen will hardly rise.

Preheat the oven to 375°F (190°C).

Bake the Stollen for 1–1½ hours, depending on size. It should be dark golden-brown. If it gets dark too early, cover it with foil. While the Stollen is still hot, brush it with melted butter until it is saturated. Once cool, cover the Stollen in plenty of confectioners' sugar and keep it in an airtight container or plastic bag for at least 3 weeks before cutting into it. It will last for several months in an airtight container.

Shown on page 163.

Zimtsterne
Cinnamon Stars

These cookies are flourless, which makes them gluten-free. Zimtsterne were my grandma's favorites, and she liked the meringue topping really thick. At home we made Zimtsterne every year; they are quick and very rewarding. A batch can be done in as little as 30 minutes. If possible, use almonds with the skin on and grind them yourself, as this way the stars get a better color and richer flavor.

*makes about 40,
depending on size of cutter*

2½ CUPS (250G) ALMONDS, GROUND (skin on)

2⅓ CUPS (275G) CONFECTIONERS' SUGAR,
PLUS EXTRA FOR DUSTING

1 TEASPOON GROUND CINNAMON

2 MEDIUM EGG WHITES

1 TABLESPOON ALMOND LIQUEUR OR RUM

Preheat the oven to 350°F (180°C). Line a baking sheet with parchment paper.

Put the almonds, 1⅓ cups (150g) confectioners' sugar and the cinnamon in a bowl and mix together. Add one egg white and the liqueur and knead with your hands until you get a smooth ball.

Dust the work surface with confectioners' sugar and roll out the dough until ½in (1cm) thick. Using a star-shaped cookie cutter of your preferred size, cut out stars and transfer them to the baking sheet.

Once you have used up all your dough, prepare the meringue topping. Using a hand mixer or a stand mixer fitted with the balloon attachment, beat the remaining egg white to stiff peaks. Add the remaining 1 cup (125g) confectioners' sugar bit by bit while whisking. Once all the sugar has been added, paint the stars evenly with meringue. The thickness of the meringue is a matter of taste, but it should cover the top of the stars and leave the sides free.

Bake the stars for 10–15 minutes. The meringue should still be white, and the stars quite delicate. They set while cooling, with a slightly chewy texture. These cookies keep very well in an airtight container and will improve over time. They will keep for at least 6 weeks.

makes 4 big hearts to write on, German funfair style, or 40 cookie-sized hearts

FOR THE STARTER
1 CUP (350G) HONEY

2½ TABLESPOONS MOLASSES

3 TABLESPOONS WATER

⅓ CUP (80G) SUPERFINE SUGAR

3 CUPS (300G) RYE FLOUR

⅞ CUP (100G) BREAD FLOUR

FOR THE DOUGH
1½ TEASPOONS BAKING AMMONIA
OR BAKING POWDER

¼ CUP (50ML) WHOLE MILK

1½ TEASPOONS BAKING SODA

1¼ CUP (150G) BREAD FLOUR,
PLUS EXTRA FOR DUSTING

2 MEDIUM EGG YOLKS

1¼ TEASPOON GROUND CINNAMON

¾ TEASPOON GROUND CLOVES

1½ TEASPOONS GROUND CARDAMOM

1½ TEASPOONS GROUND CORIANDER

¾ TEASPOON GROUND MACE

¾ TEASPOON NUTMEG

½ TEASPOON SALT

2 MEDIUM EGG WHITES, FOR GLAZING

FOR THE ROYAL ICING
2 MEDIUM EGG WHITES

4 CUPS (400G) CONFECTIONERS' SUGAR, SIFTED

LEMON JUICE, AS NEEDED

FOOD COLORING, AS DESIRED

Lebkuchen Herzen
Gingerbread Hearts

You might be familiar with the Lebkuchen hearts you can get at Christmas markets. In Germany, they are a staple at all sorts of funfairs. They have a string attached, so you can wear them like a necklace, and they are decorated with royal icing and writing, ranging from "I love you" and "for you," to wise sayings, or something silly.

These hearts have a unique, soft texture, which I love very much, resulting from a very long process and the use of rye flour. You will need at least four days to make these hearts—a real labor of love!

For the starter, put the honey and molasses in a saucepan and heat to 120°F (50°C) while stirring. Put the water and sugar into another saucepan and gently bring to a boil, stirring. Continue to boil without stirring until the sugar reaches 226°F (108°C). Let both liquids cool to about 85°F (30°C).

Once cool, mix the liquids together, then add the rye flour and bread flour. Mix well. Put the starter into an airtight container and refrigerate for at least 2 days.

To make the dough, remove the starter from the fridge and let it come to room temperature.

If using baking ammonia, dissolve it in the milk. Add the baking soda (and baking powder, if using) to the bread flour. Add the egg yolks, milk, spices, salt, and starter and mix well until the dough becomes smooth. Transfer the dough to a lined, floured baking sheet, then flatten the dough and cover. Refrigerate the dough overnight.

Preheat the oven to 450°F (230°C). Line two baking sheets with parchment paper.

Roll out the dough until ¼in (6mm) thick, using as little additional flour as possible.

Using a big heart cookie cutter 3in (7.5cm) or templates and a knife (if bigger hearts are required), cut out the Lebkuchen and transfer them to the prepared baking sheets. At this point, you also might want to make two holes to attach a string. Lightly brush with egg white.

Bake for 10–14 minutes, until dark brown. Immediately after removing the hearts from the oven, brush again lightly with egg white.

Once the hearts are cool, decorate them with royal icing. To make the royal icing, beat the egg whites until they are frothy and uniform. Fold in the sifted confectioners' sugar bit by bit. Add some lemon juice and beat the icing until it is stiff and bright white. Adjust the stiffness with additional lemon juice or confectioners' sugar. The icing should hold its shape well when piped. Add food coloring to batches of the icing, as desired, and pipe your chosen designs onto the hearts.

These Lebkuchen keep very well and should be left to improve for at least a week. They should not be hard and brittle, but rather a bit malleable. Stored in an airtight container, these will keep for several weeks.

Weisse Lebkuchen
White Gingerbread

This is a delicious old recipe with a difference. Using bread flour and superfine sugar, the crumb of this cookie remains white. The rich blend of spices, the texture, and the special glaze give it its name.

makes about 30

1¼ CUPS (250G) SUPERFINE SUGAR

2 LARGE EGGS

¾ CUP (70G) ALMONDS, SKIN ON

½ TEASPOON GROUND CINNAMON

¼ TEASPOON GROUND CLOVES

¼ TEASPOON GROUND NUTMEG

¼ TEASPOON GROUND CORIANDER

¾ CUP (130G) MIXED PEEL, FINELY CHOPPED

2 CUPS (250G) ALL-PURPOSE FLOUR, SIFTED

½ TEASPOON BAKING AMMONIA
OR BAKING POWDER

FOR THE FADENGLASUR GLAZE
⅔ CUP (125G) SUPERFINE SUGAR

¼ CUP (50ML) WATER

1 TABLESPOON RUM OR BRANDY

2 TEASPOONS CONFECTIONERS' SUGAR

FOR TOPPING
CANDIED CHERRIES

ALMONDS

This glaze is called a Fadenglasur (thread glaze) because it uses syrup that is boiled to 225°F (110°C), which in German is the Faden (thread) stage. It is a typical glaze for many types of commercial lebkuchen. You can make the glaze while the cookies are baking. Use it warm on hot cookies.

To make the glaze, put the sugar and water into a pan. Bring to a boil while stirring, and then let it boil without stirring until the syrup reaches 223°–230°F (106°–110°C). Remove the syrup from the heat. Stir in the alcohol and confectioners' sugar. Set aside.

Preheat the oven to 425°F (220°C). Line a baking tray with parchment paper.

Whisk the sugar and eggs in a large bowl until very frothy—this will take at least 10 minutes. Cut the almonds lengthwise to create almond sticks. Fold in the spices, mixed peel, and almonds. Work in the sifted flour and baking ammonia or baking powder. The dough should be stiff enough that it can be handled. Add more flour if necessary.

On a floured surface, roll out the dough into a rectangle about 1in (2cm) thick. Cut the dough into strips about 3in (8cm) wide. Cut each strip into 1in (2cm) wide strips. You will have 8 x 1in (2cm) cookies. Transfer them to the lined baking sheet, keeping about 1¼in (3cm) distance between them. Push the candied cherries and almonds into the tops of the cookies.

Bake for about 12 minutes, until light golden. Glaze them immediately using a brush before transferring them to a wire rack to cool. Stored in an airtight container, they will keep for several weeks and will improve over time.

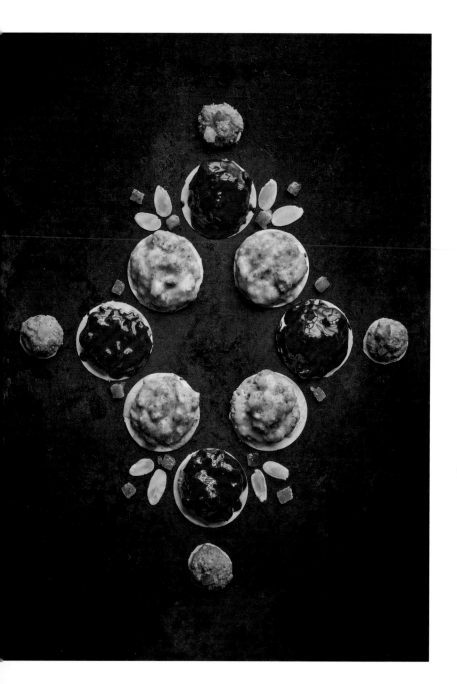

Makes 10–40, depending on size of cookies

FOR THE LEBKUCHEN
1¼ CUPS (180G)
LIGHT BROWN SUGAR, UNPACKED

5 MEDIUM EGGS

2 TABLESPOONS HONEY

2 TABLESPOONS GROUND CINNAMON

¼ TEASPOON GROUND MACE

¼ TEASPOON GROUND CLOVES

¼ TEASPOON GROUND ALLSPICE

½ TEASPOON GROUND CARDAMOM

1 PINCH SALT

2 CUPS (200G) GROUND ALMONDS

2 CUPS (200G) HAZELNUTS, GROUND

1⅓ CUP (150G) WALNUTS, FINELY CHOPPED

1½ CUPS (250G) MIXED PEEL

EDIBLE RICE PAPER DISKS
OR SHEETS (optional), AS NEEDED

Elisen-Lebkuchen
Soft Gingerbread

The best Elisen-Lebkuchen are made in Nuremberg. One of the well-known Lebkuchen bakeries uses Itaian ice-cream parlors—lying idle during the cold season—as outlets to sell their Elisen-Lebkuchen throughout Germany. Needless to say, our family was often first in the line.

The original recipes are kept secret, but I have tried to capture the taste and texture of the finest Elisen-Lebkuchen. This recipe is gluten-free.

FOR A FADENGLASUR GLAZE
¼ CUP (50ML) WATER

⅔ CUP (125G) SUPERFINE SUGAR

1 TABLESPOON RUM OR BRANDY

2 TEASPOONS CONFECTIONERS' SUGAR

FOR A CHOCOLATE GLAZE
7OZ (200G) DARK CHOCOLATE,
BROKEN INTO PIECES

3½ TABLESPOONS UNSALTED BUTTER
OR COCONUT OIL

FOR A LEMON GLAZE
1½ CUPS (150G)
CONFECTIONERS' SUGAR, SIFTED

LEMON JUICE, AS NEEDED

Preheat the oven to 350°F (180°C). Line two baking sheets with silicone sheets or parchment paper.

Beat the sugar and eggs in a large bowl until very frothy—this will take at least 10 minutes. Fold in the remaining ingredients except the rice paper. The batter should be able to hold its shape; if it is too soft, add more ground almonds.

If you are using rice paper sheets, cut them in squares or use a cookie cutter and knife to cut round wafers. The size is up to you, but around 3in (8cm) is traditional.

Portion out the batter onto the rice paper disks using a spoon or a piping bag. Transfer to the prepared baking sheets.

Bake for about 25 minutes, until dark golden in color.

If using Fadenglasur, make as directed on page 166. Apply the glaze to the hot cookies. Otherwise, leave them to cool.

To make the chocolate glaze, heat the chocolate and butter over a double boiler until melted. Apply the glaze to the cooled cookies.

To make the lemon glaze, sift the confectioners' sugar into a bowl. Add lemon juice drop by drop and stir until the glaze has the right consistency. Apply the glaze to the cooled cookies.

These Lebkuchen need to be glazed, ideally with Fadenglasur or chocolate. This way they develop a beautiful texture and flavor when left for at least 2 weeks.

Vanille-Gipfele
Vanilla Crescents

These very short and delicate cookies were always a family favorite. My grandma used to make them, and we made them in our family every year for Christmas.

They are easy and quick to make, and last very well (if you can resist eating them right away).

makes about 20 cookies

3 TABLESPOONS STRONG VANILLA SUGAR
(page 180)

½ CUP (120G) BUTTER, UNSALTED,
ROOM TEMPERATURE

1 CUP (120G) ALL-PURPOSE FLOUR

¾ CUP (80G) GROUND ALMONDS

½ TEASPOON VANILLA BEAN PASTE

1 CUP (100G) CONFECTIONERS' SUGAR,
SIFTED, FOR COATING

Preheat oven to 375°F (190°C) and line a baking sheet with parchment paper.

Combine all the ingredients except the confectioners' sugar in a bowl and work the dough with your hands until smooth.

Roll the dough into a sausage about ¾in (2cm) thick. Cut the sausage into ¾in (2cm) wide pieces. Roll each piece between the palms of your hand to get a tapered shape.

Place the cookies on the baking sheet and bend the tapered ends to get a crescent shape. Leave about 1in (2.5cm) space between the crescents.

Bake for about 10 minutes. The cookie should still be pale but start to firm up. Let the cookies cool on the baking sheet for about 3 minutes, then gently transfer to a wire rack to cool.

Once cool, toss the crescents in confectioners' sugar. Stored in an airtight container they will last for at least 6 weeks.

ME IN THE FRONT GARDEN; THE LITTLE HOUSE IN FRONT OF ME IN THIS PHOTO IS PART OF
MY EARLIEST MEMORIES.

Basics

*C*ertain cakes and other baked goods use the same components over and over again. Good examples for this are flavored sugars—vanilla sugar and cinnamon sugar. In order to keep the main recipes more readable, I decided to give these common components their own chapter.

Vanille-Zucker
Vanilla Sugar

makes 1 cup (200g)

VANILLA PODS, SPLIT OR WHOLE,
AS AVAILABLE

1 CUP (200G) SUPERFINE SUGAR,
PLUS EXTRA TO TOP OFF

In Germany, many baking ingredients are available in standardized little packets, and the recipes often list ingredients like 1 packet of baking powder, 1 packet of vanilla pudding powder, or 1 packet of vanilla sugar. This approach makes the measuring of ingredients quite easy and consistent.

In the rest of the world, this is not the case: you may be able to buy those packets in German stores or over the internet, but here is how to make a supply for yourself. Making your own vanilla sugar is very easy, and it is also a great method for storing vanilla pods, whole or split, for further use in custards and the like.

Put the vanilla pods in a tall jar that can be sealed airtight with a lid. Add superfine sugar to cover the vanilla pods completely.

Keep topping off as needed.

Luxus-Vanille-Zucker
Strong Vanilla Sugar

makes 1 cup (200g)

1 VANILLA POD

1 CUP SUPERFINE SUGAR

While the recipe for vanilla sugar makes a well flavored ingredient, sometimes you will want vanilla flavoring with a stronger punch. In those cases, use this recipe.

You might want to sift the vanilla sugar before use to remove larger bits of vanilla pod.

Cut the vanilla pod into several pieces and put it into a food processor together with about a third of the sugar. Process the sugar and vanilla pod until most of the vanilla pod has been broken down.

Put the vanilla sugar mixture into an airtight jar, together with the remaining sugar and mix. You can use this immediately, and you can keep topping off with sugar after use.

Zimt-Zucker
Cinnamon Sugar

This is such a useful and convenient ingredient to have in the cupboard for countless applications. Sprinkle it over waffles, use it to make apple sauce, to marinate apples for cake fillings, or to fill braids.

Put the ingredients into an empty jam jar. Screw the lid on and shake. Store in the jar and use as directed in your chosen recipe.

makes 1 cup (200g)

1 CUP (200G) SUPERFINE SUGAR

1 TABLESPOON GROUND CINNAMON

Apfelmus
Apple Sauce

For this I like to use a mix of sweet and sour apples, but any apple will do. It is a great way to use up apples that have become a bit unsightly.

Peel and core the apples. Cut them into chunks and place them in a small saucepan with 2 tablespoons of water.

Zest the lemon using a peeler so that you get big pieces of zest, which you can remove once the apples are cooked.

Add the lemon zest, sugar, cinnamon, and cloves to the apples. Cover the saucepan with a lid and place over medium heat. Watch the saucepan, since this mixture can easily boil over.

The apples are ready once they are all soft. Remove the zest, cinnamon, and cloves. Blend the apples.

Apple sauce can be eaten hot or cold. A portion of apple sauce with a generous dollop of sour cream is a simple dessert in its own right.

makes 7oz (200g)

5 APPLES

1 STICK CINNAMON

4 CLOVES

1 TABLESPOON LIGHT BROWN SUGAR

ZEST OF 1 LEMON

Pudding

In Germany, Pudding means a style of custard that can range from crème pâtissière to blancmange, with all sorts of flavors. The classics are vanilla and chocolate, and the vanilla version is very similar to powdered custard available in the US. Hardly anyone makes them from scratch, as Pudding Pulver (pudding powder) is readily available in shops. It is such a staple that a huge number of German recipes online, and even renowned chefs, rely on it as an ingredient.

In our family, set pudding was a favorite dessert, and it was not unusual for my mother to have ready a bowl of freshly prepared, hot vanilla—or chocolate—pudding for me after school. My grandfather loved it, too.

Vanille-Pudding
Vanilla Pudding (Without Egg)

In Germany, this kind of custard is used in many recipes, and those recipes always refer to the standardized sachets you can buy everywhere. The following recipe is a substitute for those.

makes 6–8 portions

4½ TABLESPOONS (35G) CORNSTARCH
(or potato starch)

2 CUPS (500ML) WHOLE MILK

2 TABLESPOONS SUPERFINE SUGAR
(adjust according to taste)

2 TEASPOONS VANILLA BEAN PASTE
(or 1 vanilla pod)

In a bowl, blend the cornstarch with 3 tablespoons of the milk, the sugar, and the vanilla bean paste. Bring the remaining milk to a boil in a pan. (If you prefer to use a vanilla pod, split and seed it and add both to the milk.)

Once the milk has come to a boil, whisk in the cornstarch mixture. Reduce the heat and simmer for a few minutes to cook the cornstarch. Taste to check the flavor—it shouldn't taste of starch. Remove from the heat and adjust the sugar and vanilla according to taste.

Use either as directed or pour into molds and let it set. This can be kept in the fridge for 3 days.

Luxus-Vanille-Pudding
Vanilla Pudding (With Egg)

This is richer, and more like crème pâtissière. This recipe uses starch to set the custard and to prevent the egg yolks from curdling. When the starch gets wet and heated, its molecules uncurl and interact with proteins in the egg yolk, preventing the custard from curdling

Split and seed the vanilla pod. Place both the pod and seeds, or the vanilla paste, if using this instead, in a saucepan with the milk and bring to a boil.

While the milk is heating, place the egg yolks and sugar in a bowl and beat until thick and frothy. Add the cornstarch and continue beating until well combined.

Pour a little of the boiling milk into the egg yolks, beating as you do so. Once you have a smooth mixture, pour this back into the pan of milk, beating continuously. Let it thicken and bubble a bit over low heat.

Simmer gently for a few minutes to cook the cornstarch. Taste to check the flavor—it shouldn't taste of starch. Then pour into molds to set or use as directed. This can be kept in the fridge for 3 days.

makes 6–8 portions

1 VANILLA POD
or 2 TEASPOONS VANILLA BEAN PASTE

2 CUPS (500ML) WHOLE MILK

3 EGG YOLKS

¼ CUP (60G) SUPERFINE SUGAR

4½ TABLESPOONS (35G) CORNSTARCH
(or potato starch)

Schoko-Pudding
Chocolate Pudding

The chocolate version is surprisingly easy to make, and very delicious on its own. We used to love it with canned fruit, such as peach halves or mandarin slices. While I preferred the vanilla version, my brother really loved chocolate pudding, and it is the same with my brother's kids. To this day, my mother always prepares the two flavors when she gets a visit!

makes 6–8 portions

3OZ (90G) MILK CHOCOLATE
OR DARK CHOCOLATE

1 PORTION VANILLA PUDDING
(page 184)

Melt the chocolate either in a microwave or in a heatproof bowl set over a pan of simmering water (but don't allow the bowl to touch the water). Don't let the chocolate get too hot, or it can break and become unusable. It just needs to be melted.

Use either of the recipes for vanilla pudding and prepare as directed.

Once the custard has cooled, stir in the melted chocolate.

Pour into molds to set or use as directed. Chocolate pudding keeps in the fridge for up to 3 days.

Weinschaum-Crème
Whipped Wine Custard

This custard is a bit like zabaglione, but it has developed independently in Germany. There are many recipes around. The one given here is quite simple and very tasty. You can adjust the amount of sugar depending on the wine or juice you are using.

Place all the ingredients in a bowl. Ideally, use a metal one because it conducts heat more quickly. Place the bowl on top of a saucepan of simmering water. Beat the custard until it gets frothy and thickens.

Take the bowl off the saucepan and use hot to go with Dampfnudeln (page 22) and similar dishes or pour into ramekins. Garnish with fruit and let set. This is best enjoyed within a few hours.

makes 4–6 servings

6 MEDIUM EGG YOLKS

ZEST OF 1 LEMON

2 TABLESPOONS LEMON JUICE

9OZ (250ML) WHITE WINE OR GRAPE JUICE

¼ CUP (50G) SUPERFINE SUGAR

Marzipan

Marzipan has a long history in Germany, and it is generally regarded as a delicacy. There are well-known brands making marzipan-based specialties all year round in all shapes and sizes. Lübeck is marzipan-town and Lübecker Marzipan is synonymous with the highest quality. All my family loves it, and we always looked forward to gifts of "marzipan loaves" or "marzipan potatoes" at Christmas. Marzipan is essentially a nut paste consisting of 50 percent almonds and 50 percent confectioners' sugar. It is often flavored with rose water.

Basic Marzipan

This is the standard marzipan that can be used in many recipes in this book. You can use whole almonds with skin (this is the more flavorful option) or ground almonds. Almond flour might have had its oils removed and is not suitable.

If you are using whole almonds with skins, you need to blanch them. Put the almonds into a bowl and pour boiling water over them so that they are well covered. Wait for a few minutes until the almond skins come loose, then drain and peel. Discard the skins.

Put the blanched almonds or the ground almonds into a blender and blend until they become a bit doughy. Add the rose water and confectioners' sugar and continue to blend for another 2 minutes. If the paste clings to the sides while blending, turn the blender off and use a spatula to break it up, then continue blending.

Put the almond sugar mixture into a big bowl and knead by hand until you get a smooth ball of marzipan. At this point, you can add almond flavoring or rose water to taste, if you like. If the mixture is too dry, add some more almond flavoring, rose water, or water; if it is too sticky, add more confectioners' sugar.

Wrap the marzipan ball in plastic wrap and let it rest in the fridge for at least a day. It needs this time to develop texture and flavor profile. This fresh marzipan is best used within 1 week, but will keep in an airtight container for several weeks.

makes 1¼lb (600g)

3 CUPS (300G) GROUND ALMONDS OR
10OZ (300G) WHOLE ALMONDS, ABOUT 2 CUPS

1 TABLESPOON ROSE WATER

3 CUPS (300G) CONFECTIONERS' SUGAR, SIFTED

BITTER ALMOND FLAVORING (optional),
AS NEEDED

Edel-Marzipan
Luxury Marzipan

This type of marzipan is for direct consumption, but can also be used in recipes like Stollen. Its almond content is 70 percent. You find this type of marzipan in chocolate-covered sweets of high quality. You can use whole almonds with skin (this is the more flavorful option) or ground almonds. Almond flour might have had its oils removed and is not suitable.

makes 1lb (450g)

3 CUPS (300G) GROUND ALMONDS OR
10OZ (300G) WHOLE ALMONDS, ABOUT 2 CUPS

1 TABLESPOON ROSE WATER,
ORANGE BLOSSOM WATER,
OR OTHER FLAVORING

1½ CUPS (150G) CONFECTIONERS' SUGAR, SIFTED

BITTER ALMOND FLAVORING (optional),
AS NEEDED

If you are using whole almonds with skins, you need to blanch them. Put the almonds into a bowl and pour boiling water over them so that they are well covered. Wait for a few minutes until the almond skins come loose, then drain and peel. Discard the skins.

Put the blanched almonds or the ground almonds into a blender and blend until they become a bit doughy. Add the rose water and confectioners' sugar and continue to blend for another 2 minutes. Rose water is the classic flavoring, but orange blossom water works very well, too. If the paste clings to the sides while blending, turn the blender off and use a spatula to break it up, then continue blending.

Put the almond sugar mixture into a big bowl and knead by hand until you get a smooth ball of marzipan. At this point, you can add almond flavoring to taste, if you like. If the mixture is too dry, add some almond flavoring, rose water or water; if it is too sticky, add more confectioners' sugar.

Wrap the marzipan ball in plastic wrap and let it rest in the fridge for at least a day. It needs this time to develop texture and a flavor profile. This fresh marzipan is best used within 1 week, but will keep in an airtight container for several weeks.

Hazelnut Paste

This paste can be used as a substitute for marzipan in many places. You can use whole almonds with skin (this is the more flavorful option) or ground almonds. Almond flour might have had its oils removed and is not suitable. I like to use hazelnuts with their skin on; it adds a different visual effect.

Put the almonds and hazelnuts into a blender and blend until they become a bit doughy. Add the orange blossom water and confectioners' sugar and continue to blend for another 2 minutes. If the paste clings to the sides while blending, turn the blender off and use a spatula to break it up, then continue blending.

Put the nutty sugar mixture into a big bowl and knead by hand until you get a smooth ball. If the mix is too dry, add some more orange blossom water or water; if it is too sticky, add some more confectioners' sugar.

Wrap the paste ball in plastic wrap and let it rest in the fridge for at least a day. It needs this time to develop texture and a flavor profile. This fresh marzipan is best used within 1 week, but will keep in an airtight container for several weeks.

makes 1¼lb (600g)

1½ CUPS (150G) GROUND ALMONDS OR
5OZ (150) WHOLE ALMONDS, ABOUT 1 CUP

1½ CUPS (150G) GROUND HAZELNUTS OR
5OZ (150) WHOLE HAZELNUTS, ABOUT 1 CUP

1 TABLESPOON ORANGE BLOSSOM WATER

3 CUPS (300G) CONFECTIONERS' SUGAR, SIFTED

Streusel

In German baking, streusel (the verb streuen means to sprinkle) is used in many recipes. It is typically more chunky than its American counterpart, the crumble.

makes 1½lb (650g)

2 CUPS (250G) ALL-PURPOSE FLOUR

1 CUPS (200G) SUPERFINE SUGAR

1 CUP (225G) UNSALTED BUTTER, COLD, CUBED

In a bowl, mix together the flour and sugar.

Rub the butter into flour mixture until you get a lumpy structure. German streusel is usually quite chunky.

The streusel dough can be kept in the fridge for a few hours.

Rührteig
Basic Sponge Cake

Like the classic pound cake, the Rührkuchen (stirred cake) is based on very simple ratios. The amount of flour is higher than in a pound cake or a Victoria sponge cake, which is compensated for by adding milk. The result is a sponge cake that is firm enough to hold up a fruit or streusel topping. Rührteig is widely used in German baking, and for many young home bakers, this is the first recipe they try out.

makes 1 portion

1 CUP + 1 TABLESPOON (250G)
UNSALTED BUTTER OR MARGARINE

1¼ CUPS (250G) SUPERFINE SUGAR

2 TEASPOONS VANILLA SUGAR OR
VANILLA BEAN PASTE (if desired)

4 EXTRA-LARGE EGGS

1 PINCH SALT

4 CUPS (500G) ALL-PURPOSE FLOUR, SIFTED

3½ TEASPOONS BAKING POWDER

½ CUP (125ML) WHOLE MILK

Beat the butter or margarine with the sugar and vanilla sugar (if using) until light and airy. Add the eggs and salt and beat until smooth. Add the sifted flour, baking powder, and milk and stir until all the ingredients are incorporated.

Use as directed in your chosen recipe.

About Yeasted Doughs

Yeasted dough features heavily in German baking—and in many of the baked goods in this book. I give a variety of recipes, from simple white dough to very loose and sticky, highly enriched dough. The doughs all have four ingredients in common: flour, water, salt, and yeast.

The yeast provides the leavening and needs time to do its work. Typically, it takes 2 hours or more until your cake is sufficiently risen to go into the oven, but depending on the recipe and ambient temperature, it can take much longer.

Wheat or spelt flour provides two things: starch, which makes the bulk of your dough, and gluten, which holds the dough together and traps CO_2 gas from fermentation and steam during the baking. In raw flour, there are two enzymes that react with each other when water is added to create gluten. This process can be sped up considerably by adding mechanical energy, like moving the dough or punching it. This is called kneading.

To trap gases properly and create a nice shape, the gluten needs to be organized; imagine the layers of an onion. Kneading can help organize the gluten, and that is why you shouldn't tear the dough, but, rather, stretch and fold it over itself. Good gluten development is necessary where the dough needs to hold its shape, as in breads and braids. It is not so important for cake bases of sheet cakes, for example.

I always say that yeasted dough can feel when the baker is frightened—if you don't work rapidly and with confidence, it will stick to your fingers.

Hefeteig
Basic Yeasted Sweet Dough

This basic yeasted sweet dough is very versatile and easy to work with. It can be used in cakes and tarts whenever a yeasted sweet dough is asked for. It can also be made into rolls or raisin buns. Glazing with milk or egg wash will give it a nice finish.

makes 1 portion

5 TABLESPOONS (60G) UNSALTED BUTTER, CUBED, ROOM TEMPERATURE

4 CUPS (500G) BREAD FLOUR

¼ CUP SUPERFINE SUGAR

½ TEASPOON SALT

1 X ¼OZ (7G) PACKET INSTANT YEAST, OR 2½ TEASPOONS

9OZ (250ML) WHOLE MILK, LUKEWARM

1 MEDIUM EGG

If the butter is too cold, add it to the milk and microwave or heat gently on the stovetop until the mixture is lukewarm.

Put all the dry ingredients in a bowl and beat to combine. Add the butter, milk, and egg and mix together. Then either knead by hand or use a stand mixer fitted with the dough hook. The dough is ready for proofing when it loses its stickiness and forms a smooth ball.

Cover the bowl and leave to proof for at least 1 hour, until the dough is well risen and is puffy, with lots of air bubbles. Many baking recipes mention that the dough should "double in size"—this is a somewhat unclear instruction, as the doubling could refer to the volume, or simply to the appearance of the dough, and those criteria are hard to measure.

Use as directed in your chosen recipe.

Luxus-Hefeteig
Rich Yeasted Sweet Dough

This version of yeasted sweet dough is richer and sweeter than the basic dough, and, therefore, it will be stickier and a bit more difficult to work with. Used on its own, it will make great brioche buns.

If the butter is too cold, add it to the milk and microwave or heat gently on the stove until the mixture is lukewarm.

Put all the dry ingredients in a bowl and beat until combined. Add the butter, milk, and eggs and mix together. Then either knead by hand or use a stand mixer fitted with the dough hook. The dough is very soft and sticky, and it can be a challenge to knead this by hand, so using a stand mixer is preferable. The dough is ready for proofing when it loses some of its stickiness, starts holding a ball shape, and its surface gets smoother.

Cover the bowl and leave to proof for at least 1 hour, until the dough is well risen and puffy, with lots of air bubbles.

Use as directed in your chosen recipe.

makes 1 portion

3OZ (80G) UNSALTED BUTTER, CUBED, ROOM TEMPERATURE

4 CUPS (500G) BREAD FLOUR

⅓ CUP (80G) SUPERFINE SUGAR

½ TEASPOON SALT

2¼ TEASPOONS SACHET INSTANT YEAST

1 CUP (240ML) WHOLE MILK, LUKEWARM

2 MEDIUM EGGS

makes 1 portion

4 CUPS (500G) BREAD FLOUR,
PLUS EXTRA FOR DUSTING

⅔ CUP (150ML) WHOLE MILK

2 TABLESPOONS WATER

2 SMALL EGGS, BEATEN

¼ CUP (60G) SUPERFINE SUGAR

3 TABLESPOONS UNSALTED BUTTER,
SOFTENED

2 TEASPOONS SALT

1 X ¼OZ (7G) PACKET INSTANT YEAST,
OR 2½ TEASPOONS

1 CUP + 2 TABLESPOONS (250G)
UNSALTED BUTTER,
OR MARGARINE FOR THE BLOCK

Plunder-Teig
Plunder Dough

"Plunder" is a word used in Germany for Danish pastries. They come in all kinds of shapes and with regional differences. The dough is fairly similar to croissant dough, but softer. As a result, it must be laminated at a slightly higher temperature because the consistency of the butter (or margarine) block and dough must be the same.

Put all the ingredients, except the butter for the butter block, into a bowl. Using your hands or a stand mixer fitted with the dough hook, mix well until all the ingredients are incorporated. Then knead until the dough is smooth and shows some gluten development. The dough should be fairly stiff but pliable. Add a bit more water if the dough is too stiff. Shape the dough into a square, wrap it, or put it into a square container with a lid, and leave it to proof at room temperature for 1 hour. Then refrigerate overnight.

Prepare the butter block. Soften the butter by hitting it with a rolling pin. If you use margarine, this should be soft enough.

Shape your butter block into a rectangle the size of half a letter-sized piece of paper. Use a piece of paper as your guide. Put it onto a sheet of parchment paper and fold the parchment paper so that the guide paper is fully enclosed. Replace the paper with the butter block and use a rolling pin to flatten and move the butter so that it fills the parchment paper envelope completely and has an even thickness. Refrigerate.

During the laminating process, you need to keep your butter and dough cool to ensure they have an equal consistency, and that the dough doesn't rise and puff up. Make sure the butter block and dough have a similar consistency. Roll the dough to a rectangle the size of a letter-size sheet of paper. Take the butter block out of its wrapping and place it across the middle of the dough sheet, so that the long axis of the butter block rests on the short axis of the dough sheet. Fold the uncovered pieces of dough over the butter block and squeeze them together to seal the pastry and create a seam.

Roll out the pastry in the direction of the seam, about 8in (20cm) wide and 32in (80cm) long. Now fold the pastry—first, fold both ends to the center line. If the ends are very uneven, you can trim them with a sharp knife. Then fold the pastry onto itself along the center line. This is called a book fold, for obvious reasons.

Very lightly dust the pastry with flour. Wrap the dough in plastic wrap and refrigerate it for 30 minutes or so, to let the gluten relax and the butter solidify a bit.

Next, roll out the dough along the long axis, to a rectangle of about 8in (20cm) wide and 24in (60cm) long. Fold one end to one-third over the dough, then fold the other end over to the edge, to create something like an envelope. This is often called a letter fold. Lightly dust the dough with flour, wrap, and refrigerate.

Use as directed in your chosen recipe.

Weissbrot
Basic White Bread

This is a simple, generic recipe for white bread. It is delicious, easy to make, and can be baked in all sorts of shapes and sizes, from rolls to braided loaves.

makes 1 loaf

4 CUPS (500G) BREAD FLOUR

2 TEASPOONS SALT

1¼ TEASPOONS INSTANT YEAST

1⅓ CUPS (330ML) WATER,
AT ROOM TEMPERATURE

Combine all the ingredients in a bowl and mix by hand or using a stand mixer fitted with the dough hook, until all ingredients are well incorporated. Knead for several minutes and use the windowpane test (see page 201) to determine when the dough is ready for proofing.

Cover to avoid the forming of a hard skin and leave to proof for 1–2 hours, depending on the ambient temperature and initial dough temperature. Use the poke test to check if the dough is ready for shaping (see page 201).

If using this for another recipe, continue as directed in your chosen recipe. Otherwise, divide the dough and shape as desired. Cover and leave to proof 1–1½ hours.

Preheat the oven to 475°F (245°C).

Rolls of 2½oz (70g) each need around 15 minutes, a 30oz (850g) loaf of bread of needs about 35 minutes. If baking a loaf, reduce the temperature after 15 minutes to 435°F (225°C). Keep in an airtight container for up to 5 days.

The Windowpane Test

The Windowpane Test can be used to see if a dough has been worked enough. Pick up a small chunk of dough and stretch it gently in 4 directions until it tears. If just before tearing the dough sheet is very thin and translucent (like a windowpane) it means that the gluten is well developed. If it tears while still bulky, the dough needs more kneading.

The Poke Test

Use the poke test after the first proof to check if dough is ready for shaping. Poke the dough with a finger, quick and deep. The hole should stay open and the dough should not collapse. To use the poke test to check if bread is ready to go in the oven, gently touch or poke the bread—it should feel a bit jiggly and fragile, and the dent should recover slowly.

How to shape a log with yeasted dough

Turn the dough onto a lightly floured surface. With one hand, hold the edge of the dough closest to you; with the other hand, grab the edge farthest from you and gently pull to get a flat, elongated piece of dough. Don't tear it. Fold the dough onto itself by bringing the far edge to about two thirds over the dough. Push down this edge. Using both thumbs gently, bit by bit, push this edge and the remaining single layer of dough near you under the folded part of the dough while rolling that part toward you using your fingers. This way, you should get a tight roll of dough that you can make longer and thinner by simply rolling it with the palms of your hands on the table. If the roll gets sticky, sprinkle with a bit of flour.

Index

Danke
Thank You

The book you are holding in your hands is the result of a long chain of events, and many people and organizations played their part.

First, I want to thank the team at Kyle: Judith Hannam and Emma Hanson for always having an open ear to discuss ideas and for giving me the encouragement to make the book so personal.

Thank you to the magicians who made my recipes look so good: To Maja Smend for her wizardry with light, to Lizzie Harris, Katie Marshall, and Maria Gurevich for baking and styling my recipes with great skill and creativity, and to Tony Hutchinson, who, with his sensitive choice of props, enhanced the book greatly.

To Katherine Stonehouse, my agent, you saw the possibilities in me and catalyzed the vision of books to come. You are a great guide through this world of publishing and media.

This book would not have come about without The Great British Bake Off. Thank you to the great team at Love productions, for selecting me as a contestant: You helped to elevate my skills and gave me a platform to show my baking, personality, and culture. To my fellow Bake Off bakers, I learned so much from all of you.

Developing skills and recipes for the book took time and practice. I will be forever grateful to Peter Beeby, David Gold, and all my colleagues at prospectus for giving me the space to flourish.

Along the way all my bakes needed testing and perfecting. Special thanks to the Lewes New School community who challenged my creativity and to my friends Rachel Barnard and David Seidel: You have never missed a chance to drive halfway across town to sample some of my cake and have supported me every step of the way.

And finally, I want to thank my family; the Poznanskys for their never-ending curiosity and for introducing me to Jewish culture. I feel very grateful to have married into such an inspiring group of people.

And to my parents: Mama, you gave me all your time when I was little, and my love of baking stems from those days making biscuits together around the table. Baba, thank you for letting me mess around with your huge collection of tools, taking me to the brass band, and teaching me how to take pride in good craftsmanship. Thank you both for your support and love all along the way.

Thank you to my wonderful son Benjamin, for your excitement whenever I try something new, and for your precise criticism. Bake Off and this book wouldn't have been the same without your input.

To the love of my life, Sophia: Thank you for being my wife, partner, friend, and coach: You trust me, see ways to develop my creativity which I often miss, and you bring me back down to earth whenever I get too lofty. It is a privilege to be by your side, and your contribution to this book is immeasurable.